EDUCATION FOR PEACE

EDUCATION FOR PEACE

Utopia or Reality

Dr. Pratibha Upadhyay

Education for Peace : Utopia or Reality

Rs. 650

ISBN: 978-81-7835-838-3

Published in 2010 in India by
Kalpaz Publications
C-30, Satyawati Nagar,
Delhi-110052
E-mail: kalpaz@hotmail.com
Phone : 9212729499

Laser Type Setting by: Rudra Computer Graphics, Delhi
Printed at : Chawla Offset Printers, Delhi

To,

My beloved Father-in-law, Late Dr. Shambhu Nath Upadhyay, former UNESCO Expert and Advisor, who had been a source of inspiration throughout my academic life

Contents

Preface

The world specially at the present time is in a state of utter confusion, conflicts and turmoil. In a journey to achieve the apex of material development by the techno- scientific means, we the people of modern civil society have lost our great asset called 'Peace'. Today whole world is in the grip of terror, deep sorrow and sufferings. The people's life have become so complex and miserable, that they want to get riddance from the present situation.

Accomplishment of 'Peace' is an aspiration of mankind from times immemorial, now it has been intensified. Today world community is endeavoring to establish peace intensely at the global, national, societal and individual levels. Education for Peace has been considered the best strategy to make peace in this world. The question is, whether this type of education is going to be successful in the present scenario?

Being a very small entity, a simple sensitive person and a teacher of Education, I am perplexed, How can we define the present status of the human world; chaotic, confused and turbulent? Is it the outcome of psychosocial- evolution (as social-scientists attribute it) or the result of the decline in fundamental values of life? What are the causes of human tragedy in the present modern world? What factors are responsible to throw the world in great misery? Is individual, a creator of the problems? Can the present world be transformed again into a happier and sane world by transforming individuals? Why previous efforts by world communities to make the peace in the world have failed? Have we lost our energies to understand the notion of peace and the factors associated with it? What are the means to attain peace, individually, socially and globally? Is it possible to attain peace? If Education is the last approach to build a lasting peace in the society and in the world, how can it be implemented and materialised in the present insane world? A long list of questions and my quest for the answer, inspired me to write this book, I am not an expert in the field of peace–studies, Just as a beginner and a teacher concerned with educational enterprise; I have tried my best within the premises of my limited knowledge to put and develop the idea of 'Peace', 'Education for 'Peace' and 'Peace Possibilities' in the perspective of hopes and despair pervading in the present world, in a systematic way. So many writings and ideas of socio- political and religious thinkers, educational activists, various research findings of peace studies, reports of UNESCO and various commissions in India and abroad helped me to develop and shape this book.

Now this book is to be published and would be in hands of readers, I will be thankful to almighty 'God', if my small step in the journey to 'Peace' would be beneficial and satisfying to my readers.

Dr. Pratibha Upadhyay
Professor
Department of Education
University of Allahabad

Acknowledgements

It is my duty to acknowledge my debt to those who have helped me in writing this book, First of all I salute my husband Mr. Santosh kumar Upadhyay who beared with me almost two years, of writing this book. I'm always grateful to him for he has given me ample space to grow in my life. I specially thank our dear friend Mr. R.S. Upadhyay who contributed with his comments and ideas in the initial stage of writing. I thank my friend Dr. Meenu Gupta for reading the manuscript and so generously contributing time, ideas and comments for the betterment of this book.

It will be a mistake on my part, if I don't thank my students Dr. Kshama Pandey, Buddhi Sagar, Avinash Pandey and Anamika Mishra, for their direct or indirect help in writing and shaping of this book. My heartiest thanks to my sister Prof. Vibha Upadhyay, who contributed by providing me literature relevant to my theme. My thanks to typists Anwar, Khalid and Bindeshwari Prasad for preparing the typed manuscript with great promptness and accuracy. My heart felt thanks to my children Jaya, Jyoti, Ila, Prashant and Shashank who sporadically contributed by their help throughout writing.

Last not the least, I am extremely thankful to my friend Dr. Saroj Pandey who perhaps made, me enter the gateway of

'Think Peace' by inviting me in a experts workshop in NCERT, New Delhi. It was the first step of my journey to Peace. Now I have long way to go. In the end, my deepest gratitude goes to all those thinkers and experts of Peace Studies from whom I received valuable ideas in writing this book.

Finally, I thank 'God' who has given me strength to complete this book.

Dr. Pratibha Upadhyay

Introduction

Education for peace is not a slogan or catchword that has been coined recently in this world but more precisely it emerged as a trend and an urgent call of world community around First World War. The people realised that education was the only means to regain peace in the world after the catastrophe of war. Since then, education has been tried several times but unfortunately failed. After the World War II creation of United Nations and its agencies like UNESCO was nothing but to establish peace in the world by educating minds of people. So much so the noble andeavour never fully succeded because of the lack of will and commitment of people on one hand and the its utopian nature on the other. However, struggle to make peace through education continued and never stopped. Even today efforts are still going on in one way or other throughout the world and it should go until such world is achieved or until all human civilisation perishes in some further war and battles of unthinkable ferocity.

1

Human Miseries in The Modern World : Peace a Lost Paradise

The human miseries and pains were always there in the history of mankind, only their nature changed with the period of time. Today in the modern civilized world, where material development has crossed all boundaries man is moaning in pain that has been never before. What are the pains and miseries of modern human society and what are the factors which are responsible for destroying the peace of human beings? Who are the creators of sufferings and sorrow may be best portrayed by various deadly and injurious events which have occurred and are still occurring in the history of mankind.

Today, on one hand human civilisation has reached the apex of material development due to techno-scientific progress and on the other, human society has become a victim of war, and weapons of mass destruction, terrorism, environmental destruction, population menace, poverty, food and hunger, illiteracy, over politicisation of human civil society, globalisation, marketisation, moral decay of human being and consequent psycho-physical diseases.

In the modern world violence in various forms and the complex forces unleashed by techno-scientific development have transformed the people into miserable and restless creatures on this earth. A blind race of material development compounded with nuclear armament of nations and global terrorism have ruined the tranquility of human lives. Today where is 'peace'; for which humanity has been aspiring from times immemorial? We are to seek it in the midst of human miseries manifested through contravening forces unleashed in this world at national and international levels.

War, Terrorism and Genocide

Today, we are living in the world of international terrorism and warfare. Humanity is under the threat of nuclear holocaust and is standing on a precipice where only one step forward is sure to throw it into a bottomless pit from where the rays of life would hardly be discernible. Never before in the history of mankind, war had been so hideous, terrible and devastating as it has become today as advanced bio-chemical and nuclear weapons of mass destruction can wipe out the human civilization in no time. The destruction unleashed in the Hiroshima bomb is estimated as only a millionth of the destructive power of the weapons of mass destruction (WMD) today.

The nature of war has been changed, war is not limited to battlefields or national boundaries rather it has taken the form

More wars are caused by bad- tempered people seeking to discuss peace propositions than by good tempered people seeking to discuss war measures.

Dr. Josshiah old field of London (a speech given on the eve of the Second World War)-

of guerilla war or the proxy war where the agents of enemies and terroristts groups create devastation amidst the civilian population of the countries.

In recent years we have experienced the frightful and devastating events in the history of mankind as : gruesome attack 9/11 (2001) on American Trade Centre (New York, U.S.A), terrifying invasions in Afganistan and Iraq, serial bomb blasts in Mumbai, Delhi and other part of India, U.K. Pakistan and so many other countries. Specially the recent terriflying and awful episode 26/11 (2007) in Mumbai created by terrorist group has entered the dictionary of terror, when terrorists laid sieze to the city's roads, airports, railway station, hospitals and two of its best known luxury hotels, leaving a trail of death and destruction.[1]

The people of India and the world alike witnessed the scenes of devastating explosions, raging fires, dead bodies, heavily armed terrorists firings indiscriminately at people on the streets and a metropolis on the knees[2] through media.

The rockhurling event of terrorism trembled not only India but the whole world and specially those countries whose common citizens and high profile people were the victims of the naked dance of violence and brutality. The open terror drama was the most organised terrorist act by the international terrorist group probably the Pakistan based Lashkar-e-Taiba and orchestrated by Al-Queda.

Presently, terrorism not only international but also territorial is one of the most dangerous and pernicious threat to human survival. Everyday acts of terrorism are freshened in the minds of people. The whole world is living under the dreadful shadow of national and international terrorism and prospective war. The countries which back terrorists and terrorists organizations are also subjected to their own deeds and have ruined the lives of their own people. These countries are; Iran, Syria, Libya, Cuba, North Korea, Sudan, Afghanistan (as listed by U.S.) and Pakistan (as India perceived).[3] The people of these countries are victims of economic collapse , poverty, starvation, and are lacking social security and various types of services as health and education. They are even deprived of the 'right to live', in Pakistan, bomb-blasts and destruction by terrorists have become the order of the day. Within the Indian territory, there are number of terrorist and separatist groups, who are active in creating terror, violence and destruction, some of which are: United Liberation Front (ULF), People's Liberation Army and National Council of Nagaland in Northeastern India, Khalistan Guerilla Force, Khalistan Liberation Force, Khalistan Liberation Front, Babbar Khalsa, Khalistan Liberation Army and Maoist group etc in North India, Lashkar-e-Taiba, Jaish-e-Mohammed, Al-Queda and Harkat-ul-Mujahideen etc in Kashmir. Peoples War Group, Balbir Militias, Ranvir Sena and Naxals in Central India.[4] Today, terrorism is the biggest threat to human life and greatest violation of the human right to live.

In the modern history of mankind there are several examples of genocides which have been caused by wars and terrorism. After World War II, the Nazi holocaust was seen as a unique case of genocide, which tolled the death of 60,00,000 people. What Adolph Hitler declared to his army commanders on August 22, 1939 was,

"Thus for the time being I have sent to the east only my 'Death Head Units' with the orders to kill without pity or mercy all men, women and children of polish race or language, only in such a way will we win the vital space that we need. Who still talks nowdays about the Armenians?[5]

At present, terrorism is a biggest security threat to man as an individual and mankind as a whole. How can a modern man live in peace in the midst of terror and insecurity. After the World War II, there are several examples of genocides apart from Nazi holocaust as Poll Pot in Cambodia (1975-1979), Rwanda (1994) & Bosnia-Herzegovina (1992-1995), which tolled the deaths of millions of people. Today mass murders and genocide of different communities are still going on in one or other parts of the globe.

In India, genocide of Kashmiri Pandits and Kashmiri Hindu community is still taking place and they are facing terrible plights after mass exodus. Terrorists in the state massacred large number of Kashmiri Hindus and more than three lakhs internally displaced Kashmiris were hounded out of their native homes.[6]

Environmental Destruction

Today, man has conquered the natural resources by means of science and technology and has rapidly achieved the apex of the material development of human civilization. In the blind race of not only material development but of nuclear armament, a delirious man has forgotten the future sustenance of human life on this earth.

With growth in population and increased unbanisation, the lifestyle of people in the modern civil society has undergone drastic change in the developed countries as well as in the developing countries. Consequently all sectors of the human population have been cut off from the close contacts, they had so far maintained with natural environment. This has been described as a divorce between man and nature brought about

Nature provides a free lunch, but only if we control our appetites.

William Ruckelshaus

by the victory of science and technology over nature. Today, population explosion with the desire for better living conditions and greater consumption of material goods have placed an unprecedented strain on the considerable, but nevertheless limited resources that nature offers us.[7]

Due to imperfect understanding of natural systems and mechanisms which make possible the maintenance of life on the earth; disregard of unintentional effects of technology, in particular the various forms of pollution; poor management of the soil, forest and water; unbridled consumption of fossil fuels, uncontrolled urbanization; the relegation of the rural population to a marginal position ; destruction of the existing background to life and crushing of traditional cultural values, man has reached a point of historic environmental crisis.[8] The techno-scientific economy of modern world has terribly added to destruction of the environment.

Not only this, there is ultimate evil which has destroyed the global environment beyond imagination, that is nuclear detonation by different nations of the world participating in the race of nuclear armament. This is the greatest threat to the survival of mankind on the planet earth. Presently, Nuclear Weapon States as; United States, Russia, France, United Kingdom, and China have sufficiently large stockpiles of nuclear weapons (active or inactive) and fissile materials which are to be cleared and recycled but are not disassembled even today. Other than these states, India, Pakistan, and North Korea are the countries who have been testing nuclear weapons

Ours is a world of nuclear giants and ethical infants. We know more about war than we know about peace, more about killing than we know about living. We have grasped the mystery of the atom and rejection the Sermon on the Mount.

Omar N. Bradley-

successively just to establish themselves as nuclear weapons states and become a member of the "Nuclear Club". India and Pakistan are the strong contestants in the nuclear armament race in the Asian region. Today India has succeeded and has become a member of the "Nuclear Club".[9]

As history witnesses, India has always stood for non-violence and peace in the world. It is rather the spirit of India as a nation. But in due course of nuclear armament race, it has prepared itself for the defence from nuclear warfare. Today, India is sufficient in Nuclear, Biological and Chemical infrastructure and facilities to produce NBC weapons and to meet the challenges of most advanced Nuclear, Biological and Chemical warfare. The tendency of armament among nations is the outcome of regional insecurity and balance of power. This is also called mutually assured destruction (MAD).

Moreover, nuclear weapons and fissile materials are smuggled across the territories of countries by terrorist groups and are used in creating mass destruction of human lives and the environment as a whole.

Nuclear detonation in the form of air bursts, surface bursts and subsurface bursts create a severe environment including blasts, thermal pulses, neutron, X and gamma rays, radiations, electromagnetic pulses and ionization of the upper atmosphere of the earth. The effects are manifested as ground shock, water shock, "blue out" cratering, large amount of dust and radio-active fallouts. All pose problems for the survival of friendly eco-system and lead to the destruction or neutralisation of hostile assets. Blasts and shocks are virtually the most effective destruction mechanism for the environment, their effects on the atmosphere are experienced beyond the thousands of kilometers from their own territory.[10]

In this way, nuclear detonation imposes sufferings of the most horrible kind on their victims including on the yet unborn through trans generational effects. Who can forget the first nuclear detonation by America on Japan during World War II It was the greatest nuclear holocaust, that was witnessed in the history of humanity

Today, nuclear weapons are million times stronger than what America used in World War II. Their capacity of mass destruction is unimaginable. Civil and medical defense against them is impossible. They are uniquely "evil" in their capacity to exterminate all life on this planet. The International Court of Justice has called them "The ultimate evil".[11] So, humanity is facing disastrous effects of environmental destruction as, soil erosion, decreasing underground water, depletion of ozone layer; green house effects, air and water pollution, and last but not the least, global warming.

It is universally accepted that global warming is a real threat and not a figment of some scientist's imagination. It will unleash catastrophic consequences ranging from an increase in violent storms to severe droughts, crops failure, rising sea level, massive floods worldwide, increasing evidences of infectious diseases, death from heat waves and loss of fragile species on earth are some of the many perils. It could spell disaster for all lives on the earth, the planet that we call home.

India still a developing country is most affected by environmental changes. The turbulent climatic change is going to create havoc with our economy which is still greatly dependent on farming and agriculture. Recently India has faced massive floods in rivers in different states like Bihar, Orissa

I think the environment should be put in the category of our national security. Defence of our resources is just as important as defence abroad otherwise what is there to defend?

Robert Redford

and Uttar Pradesh. The sufferings of the affected people are beyond imagination.

It is forecasted that in very near future, a large scale effect of affore- mentioned environmental destruction is possible, if we, the people of the world, are not going to be conscious of the hazardous consequences of our pernicious interactions with nature. There is a great question of survival and sustenance of modern man and his future generations to come in the unsafe and injurious environment. Consequently, in the present perilous atmosphere the main source of unhappiness and fear in human beings is the major health threat to them.

Health Threats and Diseases

Today there is a class of people who are exposed to the modern lifestyle developed by the techno-scientific progress of human civilization. They have gathered "means" of luxury and comfort in their lives. Thus their luxurious style life combined with hazardous environment is causing severe health problems to them. Besides there are masses who are poor and are being killed by the diseases caused by their unhygienic living conditions, malnutrition and starvation.

However in general, due to climate change, various types of pollutions and global warming, people are suffering from chronic and fatal diseases. Heart ailments, Diabetes, Asthma, various types of allergies, Cancer and Hepatitis have become common in the modern world; Malaria, T.B. and other diarrhoeal diseases are taking their toll in large numbers but the greatest threats that the world has been facing is, that of cancer and AIDs epidemics. HIV/AIDS is the major challenge with implications beyond the health sector and socio-economic factors. Global warming is playing havoc not only with the physical health of people but is causing mental diseases as well.

Another perplexing situation, mankind is facing today, is population explosion, which is also the most basic cause of environmental destruction and unhappiness in people. A speedy growth in population has created menace in the world.

Population Menace

The population in world is growing with leap and bounds and creating a threat to human survival. The overgrowth of population, specially in developing and undeveloped countries, has outstripped the provision of housing, food, safe drinking water, health care services, education, youth employment, power supply, and so on so forth. Population explosion has increased demand on water and energy exponentially. It is predicted that the next world war will be fought for water. The population growth directly and indirectly causes the environmental pollution and destruction.

Not only this, demographic imbalance has become a major challenge to the modern human society. Particularly in India due to social taboos, sex determination, female fetocides and infanticides are rampant and are causing the decline in male – female ratio. This trend is very dangerous and in near future it is going to induce very serious moral and ethical problems in the society. If it is not restrained, it will definitely destroy the ethical and moral fabric of the Indian society. The repercussion of this trend is being perceived in our Indian society even at present. This is a matter of anxiety, because decrease in female population implies an increase in sexual crimes and abuses. If this trend is not stopped, the future of Indian society and its Constitution is at stake. The next cause of misery in Indian society is the community oppression and discrimination due to which, a large segment of Indian population is not at peace rather they are leading a miserable life. Not only in India, but in other countries also racial and sex discrimination are also prevalent.

Community Oppression and Discrimination

Oppression of the Backward and Dalit classes of the Indian Society is still continuing in different parts of the country. Despite the Constitutional and legal provisions, the Scheduled Tribes are deprived of the minimum level of subsistence as the higher caste has been an obstacle in their progress. The legal and political system too, provides affirmative discrimination which is in their favour.[12]

Scheduled Tribes are the last marginal people who lag behind even the Scheduled Castes for their century old isolation from upper caste led civilisation. However, both the communities are a common victim of caste discrimination. Nowdays Dalit politics has drawn the nation-wide attention and is gaining power in the parliamentary system of democratic India, but very few of them are enjoying the fruits of their struggle. The majority of the backward classes is still the sufferer of inequality and social and economic discrimination in the society.

Today, a large segment of the Dalit and Backward population is still deprived of food, shelter and minimum standard of life. They still exist in conditions where they are economically oppressed, starved or in miserable health. This may be called violence on part of them. Violence is expressed not only in battlefields but also through circumstances which limit the life, civil rights, health, individual freedom and self fulfillment. This type of violence referred to as the structural violence which occurrs when wealth and power exploit or oppress others. The structural violence implies those situations where individual's survival is threatened and are not peaceful. In India, the problem of poverty is the result of age old 'structural violence'. Not only in India, but there are several developing and underdeveloped countries like Somalia, Ethiopia, Latin

America and African countries where a mass of the population is living under poverty and miserable conditions, how can we expect 'peace' in the world.

Next oppressed class in the world is 'women'. Today, it is needless to say that a class of women have achieved the apex positions in the society. they are excelling in every field of human life and competing with their male counterparts. There are several examples in the world and also in India itself, which show the empowerment of women. The recent foremost example is our first woman president of India Smt. Pratibha Patil, other empowered women are Mrs. Sonia Gandhi, Ms. Mayawati and lots of women, who are politically strong. As history indicates Mrs. Indira Gandhi was the most powerful woman of the country and the world as well.

In various fields, some of the examples of women who have surpassed their male counterparts are Mrs. Kiran Bedi in police and social service, Mahashweta Devi and others in literary fields, Miss Barkha Dutta in journalism and media; there are women who are CEOs and are heading various multinational companies and industries; not only this, there are women who are serving in armed forces and other defence services in the capacity of senior officers. But such women constitute a small proportion of our female population and most of them still feel insecure and exploited in their work place by their male counterparts. They are not safe psychologically and physically in the male dominated world. Other than the so called empowered class of women, the story is not the same for rest of the women population. It is sad to see that even today, a large population of women not only in rural and backward areas but in urban cities and metros are still facing domestic and social violence. Not only in India, in every part of the world they are facing physical and mental abuses. Everyday in one part or the other, women are beaten, molested, raped and killed by men.

All forms of violence against women and girls, whether physical, sexual, psychological should be seen as the gross violation of women's right to live a dignified life in the world. Is this not the greatest misery of woman life today. When would they breathe freely in this men's world, is a dream.

Another great evil, being faced by India specially is, over politicisation of every aspect of our Indian social life. Today, politics has ruined the social fabric of Indian society. Whatever agitations, fermentation and restlessness are seen everyday, are mostly due to over politicisation of the problems of social life. What does it mean, we have to see.

Over Politicisation of Human Life

The development of political consciousness in the people of democratic setup is healthy and necessary but over politicisation of every aspect of human life is very dangerous. Particularly in India, after independence, a class of people are being produced and their population is growing tremendously day by day, who are called politicians. Millions of them are coming from every nook and corner of Indian society and have over politicised the functioning of the democratic system. History teaches us that, if a nation is governed by too much politics, it is bound to wither and die. Too much politics destroys the quality of politics as much as the moral tone of man and shatters the fabric of human society. This is the reason why India is going down morally day by day.[13]

Today people are coming in politics not for serving the society and nation, rather for the sheer pursuit of power and nothing but power and they are gaining so much from power without any concern for the society and nation. All political parties have lost their credibility amidst the people of India.

Today our constitutional provisions for social justice are reduced to mere slogans by the political parties in searching the shortcuts to political power. The constitutional provisions for Scheduled Castes, Scheduled Tribes and Backwards are misused and misinterpreted by our political parties to establish their vote banks. This tendency has aroused powerful passions among different groups of politicians leading to violent clashes among them.

Today, in politics, ideological warfare have been diluted in the name of coalition governments. Somehow or the other, political parties gather to form coalition governments with common minimum programmes but this arrangement does not work and implies the unstability in the governance.

Over politicisation of thoughts has led agitation and social fermentation rather dilemma in the society. This situation is not only in India but throughout the world. There is a crisis of ideology which has created the present chaotic situation or anarchy in the democratic and social system of India. This is the tyranny of excessive politics. Generally our governments are led by so called leaders who are mafias, dons, dacoits and people with muscle and money. In politics, very few are genuine people but they are not organised and hence not effective. On the whole, country is suffering from the diseases of cynical, misdirected and unconcerned (with the welfare of people and nation) politics ; this implicates unstability of governments; no development work can be undertaken successfully in the premises of chaotic situation prevailing in the governing machinery. Modern political scenario, specially in India, is frustrating and painful for the people who are sensitive enough to think. A great question confronting us is, whether political environment in our country is conducive for the peaceful living of its members?

Globalisation, Marketisation and Human Psyche

Techno-scientific development of human society, revolution in Information Technology (IT), extension of markets beyond the boundaries of nations, international trade and over act of media have made the world globalise. Man has overcome the hurdle of distance due to cyber transportation; he can get any information within a fraction of second by the grace of IT. No doubt, www (world wide web) has really made the society a web of connections among individuals, hence one can say that, the modern term 'globalisation' is synonymous to the Indian concept of 'Vasudhaiva Kutumbakam'. But in real sense of terms 'Vasudhaiva Kutumbakam' is a moral term which implicates the collectiveness, belongingness and unification of society as a whole while the modern concept of globalisation is merely a commercial term which implicates the international trade, growth of market and consumerism.

It is needless to say that globalisation has created opportunities for not only the extension of markets and international trade but the provisions of education and job opportunities across the boarders. A large population of youth is getting jobs in call-centers and Multi National Companies (MNCs) situated in metro cities with lucrative pay-packages while there is mass of educated unemployed and underemployed youths from small cities and towns who are struggling for respectful jobs with salaries much less than that of pay-packages of MNCs. Though MNCs and call centrs are paying handsome salaries to youngsters, but the unfortunate part of this trend is manifested through the victimisation of young lots by the work culture of these multi nationals. Today the style of working in call centers and software companies is causing serious health hazards to their young employees. The economic recession in the world market causes serious threat to job opportunities for the prospective youths; not only this, it creates horrific situations

Like population explosion, the consumptions explosion can not continue much longer, it is inherently self defeating process.

Julian Muxley- (Evolution after Darwin)

for youngsters who are already serving in various industries. In the present world of manipulative market, people have lost job securities, so how can these youngsters be expected to remain in peace with hammering uncertain future. Apart from uncertainty of future among young people, the modern trend of globalisation has widened the gap and created disparity in the society, rather it has created artificial demands and desires in the modern men.

Today an individual, a society and a nation is rated as consumer in the global market. Unnecessary and over growth of markets of not only goods but also of human capabilities and traits have increased the degree of competitions in the society. The trend of unhealthy competitions has thrown our people specially the younger generation into psychological crisis.

The people are fascinated by the dazzling markets and trendy malls and hence, are becoming the prey of unrestricted desires which can't be fulfilled by their limited means. In this way, present scenario of the markets have made man extremely materialist without any spiritual and ethical backing. In the present global world, due to cut throat competitions, materialistic approach towards life and multiplied desires, negative emotions as : fear, insecurity, anger, disgust, lust, loneliness and mental depression are precipitating in day to day lives of people, in particularly younger generation and thereby pushing them into psychological trauma.

Everyday, our minds are freshened by the news of suicide, murder, rape, mental depression and so many types of agitations in youths. Educational campuses are no exceptions. Today the education sector is in the grip of corrupt people; all types of

The truth is that the state is a conspiracy designed not only to exploit, but above all to corrupt its citizens.

Leo- Tolstoy- (a letter to his friend V.P.B. Bottkin)

malpractices, nepotism and dishonesty are present in educational enterprises. Education today, is completely commercialised. Globalisation has enhanced the pressure on educational institutions, specially on the universities, to prepare their students for global markets. Universities are unable to cater to the demands of young people, hence the self financing institutions are mushrooming in every nook and corner to fulfill their demands. These institutions are actually exploiting youngs for their dreams to come true. This trend has increased the population of under-employed youth in our society and consequent frustration among the young generation. Today in the global scenario, where our young generation is restless, insecure and agitated how can we expect peace in the society.

More Further, the inevitable and intense contribution of globalisation is the role of media, which is enhanced by leaps and bounds by the grace of information technology. Today positive role of media can not be over looked where it is arousing and awakening the people to react to various gross afflicting problems and situations, the world is confronting with. But at the same time, it's role is terrific, it has entered the living rooms of people with packages of uncensored news and programmes in the name of 'free flow of information and freedom of expression'. Various news channels are glamourising the news regarding the acts of terrorism and other evil and wicked deeds in the society to increase their TRPs. The presentation as reality shows by media is more terrifying than the actual incidences. So besides providing information, media is adding fear and insecurity among the people. It is deculturing the society as well. Perhaps, the modern trend of globalisation and marketisation seems to be irreversible, hence one has to seek his own path to peaceful living. Other then the aforementioned factors which are affecting people negatively, the greatest malady of modern life is the general moral decay of the society.

Moral Maladies

Moral decay is the serious disease of modern society. World wide human society in general and Indian society in particular is going down morally day by day. Today man has accumulated wealth, power and means of luxury but has lost his moral strength which is a necessary condition for his sustenance.

The English poet Oliver Gold Smith had warned,

"Ill fare the land to hastening ills a prey,

Wealth accumulates and men decay"

In India, our masses (poor) had never decayed in the age old poverty to same extent as our classes (rich people) have decayed in their wealth during this post independence period.[14]

Today the moral decay of our classes have been, filtered down to our masses as well. The moral maladies of our Indian society are manifested through gross selfishness, uninhibited dishonesty, exploitation, bribery, corruption, malpractices of all sorts in politics, industries, business, police, education and even in defence services. Above all, the erosion of mutual trust and confidence is seen even in the pledge words of our people. The moral crisis reveal the spiritual and ethical bankruptcy of our people today.[15]

India is growing into an industrial and economic giant and competitor of the global market but remains a moral pigmy, with millions and millions of people steeped in poverty and

War, huge military expenditures, waste of resources pollution, diseases and national disasters are the enemies of the human race against which all people can direct aggressive tendencies.

Ronal J. Glossop, (Confronting War : An Examinations of Humanity's Most Pressing Problem)-

squalor in between. Moreover there is also a great malady of modern life: The invasion of the philosophy of permissiveness in the society in general. Since the Second World War, this philosophy invaded throughout the developed World, and entered slowly in the eastern nations as that of ours, India. The philosophy of permissiveness in its extreme form has destroyed the soul of the people concerned, destroyed also their happiness and peace.

Today more and more people are afflicted with the craze for organic cravings and satisfactions unchecked and undisciplined; they seek only pleasure, more pleasure and still more pleasure. Sex, violence, drunkenness and similar evils are creeping into the society; vulgarity has become a fashion today. Thus, sheer pursuit of unchecked individual pleasure, uninspired by any standard of ethical and moral values, is lowering the quality of human life and human tastes step by step and bringing the ruin of family, the ruin of a society, the ruin of whole civilisation.

This is a very dangerous situation. In the absence of ethical and spiritual discipline, society becomes spiritually weakened; all sorts of evils enter the society by which the society decays and finally dies. Here is a great example of the history of Roman Empire and civilization which decayed and died of this permissive philosophy, about which Edward Gibbon has told vividly in his famous book: "Decline and Fall of the Roman Empire".[16]

In this way, present day global needs and diverse scenarios of violence and NBC (Nuclear, Biological and Chemical) weapons, depletion of resources, pollutions, terrorism, increase in moral maladies and promiscuity in modern civil society, balance of terror and mutual suspicions among peoples

Unless men increase in wisdom as much as in knowledge, increase of knowledge will increase sorrow.

Bertrand Russell (Import of science on Society)

and nations alike, are pricking human society extensively. Hence, the world is in a sorry mess and India is too. This is the most difficult period in the history of mankind which has aroused a question of survival and sustenance of human life. So, how shall we bring order out of this chaotic and sorrowful condition prevalent in the whole world? How can we achieve true human welfare and tranquility amidst the miseries of modern human society? Is it possible to find remedy of human miseries today? If it could be possible, why United States and other G8 countries are the lowest in Happiness Index (Happy Planet Index, HPI launched by NEF)[17] in the world, while they are most resource efficient, and affluent societies in every manner as Human Development Index (education, health and richness) indicates.[18] Why people of these countries are miserable and lonely? This is the perplexing question humanity is encountering with. This is not the question of present but a question which has been asked for millennia. Our saints and philosophers as Buddha, Mahavira, Gurunanak, Sufi saints and seers in India, Greek philosophers, such as Aristotle strived to seek the answers of the question. Aristotle thought of the ultimate end or good, as something that should be strived for in its own right. Aristotle proposed that people's happiness was the highest good and his understanding of happiness embraced living and doing well, not just feeling good. This is why the US Declaration of Independence entrenched the pursuit of happiness as a fundamental right for all citizens of the new country.[20] The questions is, has America achieved happiness through material development and affluences? The answer is shockingly 'no'. Omar Bradely, US General says, "Ours is a world of nuclear giant and ethical infants" hence, it is believed that 'happiness is not related with physical or material development. Happiness lies in 'peace' or tranquility in the minds and inner self of the individuals and in the harmonious state of the world as a whole. 'Peace' is a paradise or heaven, every human being and society aspires to live in, but where is it?

A modern poet , philosopher, a thinker Gurudeva Ravindra Nath Tagore sung a song offered to Almighty, aspiring for such a heaven;

> Where the mind is without fear
> and the head is held high;
> Where knowledge is free,
> Where the world has not been
> broken into fragments
> by narrow domestic walls;
> Where words come out from
> the depth of truth;
> Where tireless striving stretches
> its arms towards perfection;
> Where the clear stream of reason
> has not lost its way
> into the dreary desert sand
> of dead habits;
> Where the mind is led forward
> by thee into ever widening
> thought and action
> Into that heaven of freedom
> my Father let my country awake.[21]

Gurudeva Tagore aspired for that heaven of freedom where all can live in delight without fear. Tagore's quest for heaven seems to be a divine inspiration as Jesus Christ says, "The kingdom of Heaven is within us.[22] The kingdom of heaven is nothing but the inner peace or tranquility in every human being, which is the outcome of interaction of individual with his outside world.

We seek peace, knowing that peace is the climate of freedom.

Dwight D. Eisenhower-

Tagore's aspiration for heaven is nothing but the quest for environment where a man or society can live freely in peace and harmony without fear.

However, peace is the lost paradise amidst the miseries of modern world. Is it possible to regain? It is an eternal question.

References

1. Bhupta, M, and Pai. A. (2008), New Terror Strategy, *India Today*, Dec. 8.
2. *Ibid.*
3. From Wikipedia.
4. List of terrorist gropus, http//en. wikipedia.org/wiki
5. http//www.history place.com
6. Hejela, R & Hajela. R (2005), "Human Rights and Human Survivial,' *Human Rights, Emerging Issues,* Allahabad, published by Innovative Research Association. p. 59.
7. Unesco Report (1977), *Thinking ahead, Unesco and the challenges of today and tomorrow,* p. 265.
8. *Ibid.*
9. List of states with nuclear weapons. http//en. wikipedia.org/ wiki
10. Estimatyed World Wide Nuclear Stockpile, http//en. wikipeida. org
11. *Ibid.*
12. Hajela & Hajela, op.cit. p. 65.
13. Ranganathanada (1986), *Esternal Values for A Changing Society*,Bombay, Bhartiya Vidya Bhawan, Vol. III, p. 349.

14. *Ibid*, p. 422.

15. *Ibid,* p. 97.

16. *Ibid*, pp. 368-74.

17. THE (un) HAPPY PLANET INDEX, An index of, human well being And environmental impact, published by n.ef (the new economic foundation) Friends of Earth, 2008 http//en.wikipedia.org./wiki/Happy Planet Index.

18. Human Development Index. Form wikipedia.http//en.wikipedia.org./wiki/Happy Planet Index.

19. THE HAPPY PLANET INDEX, *ibid.*

20. *Ibid.*

21. Ravindra Nath Tagore, Gitanjali (35).

22. Ranganathananda, op.cit. p. 307.

2

Oh, Peace! What Is It?

The fast track material development of human civilisation has dehumanised the man. Today, humans are so restless and miserable that, they have lost their energies and wisdom to realise and sensitise the feeling of 'peace'. They are not even able to identify and comprehend the factors which cause the induction of peace in an individual, society, nation and in the world. Thus it has become inevitable today, to know what peace is and what the principles of being in peace are. Before understanding the state of being in peace, we have to deal with the question, what 'peace' is!

Is peace mere absence of war or violence? Or is it something we strive for but have not really experienced? Is it something that can not be fully achieved but can only be approached? Or is it something that begins with an individual? Is it then something that is to be acquired and shaped? Or is it a binding emotion which is an inherent part of any culture and

Peace is not the absence of war; it is a virtue; a state of mind; a disposition for benevolence; confidence; and justice.

Spinoza:

human society to survive? Answers to all questions about peace confronting us, may be well organised in the form of concept and meaning of peace.

Concept and Meaning of Peace

As far as the concept of 'Peace' is concerned, it has changed throughout history of mankind as individuals and different groups have struggled to realise a harmonious state of existence.[1] Many people think of peace as the absence of war or violence or conflict. Some think, 'peace' as a state of tranquility in an individual or in the environment. But in a comprehensive term 'Peace' is a positive concept which implies much more than the absence of war or violence or conflict rather it is the practice of love and necessary condition for human survival.[2] When Jesus said, "Love Thy Neighbour As Thy Self", neighbour does not mean the physical or close relation rather it is extended to all levels of human beings and creatures surrounding us.[3] Hence, the last line of 'Peace Chant' (Santi Patha, Katha Upanishad) which is important and significant in this connection may also be quoted : ***'ma vidvisavahai'. Om Santih, Santih, Santih*** —'let us not hate each other'. Hate is the product of a sense of human separateness and is a fellow traveller with fear, tension, exploitation and violence. Hence we should refrain from 'hate' for being at Peace, Peace and Peace.

Some people say, peace is an ontological principle concerning the humanising of human beings. It is an attitude towards life which by restraining violence, strengthens social cohesion and makes life worth living.

Peace is not some thing that we can achieve at some point and neglect it thereafter, it has come to be treated as a precondition of survival, growth and development, of mankind.[4]

Peace is not merely a distant goal that we seek but a means by which we arrive at the goal.

Martin Luther King Jr. -

Ian M. Harris (1988) explains the concept of peace as; "Peace' is a concept which motivates the imagination, connotes more than the cessation of war, implies human beings working together to resolve conflicts, respect standards of justice, satisfy basic needs and honour human rights."[5]

On the whole, Peace has different meanings in different contexts, so it can be appropriately defined and understood, only in those contexts.

Individual Context

Peace has individual context which implies tranquility or calmness in the mind and heart of an individual. In very simple language, for an individual to live peacefully, he or she must be able to satisfy basic needs and resolve conflicts within family, friendships, work place and community in such a way that promotes the well being of all.

When a person learns to practice, certain principles of life as love, compassion, patience, forgiveness, truthfulness, control on desires, greed, passion and anger along with the skills of arbitrating conflicts and negotiating agreements, he tends towards peace. Swami Ranganathananda says, "Fear, tension and all types of negative emotions disappear when the ego of individuality grows into the ego of personality".[6] It is dimension of spiritual growth that makes man develop the capacity to integrate oneself with others in society, to live at peace with others. The growth of individuality into personality is infact inward journey of man which the Gita calls by simple word 'Yoga'. A man develops a new quality, impart a new value system to his life, which manifest through his expressions of the human responsibility, a responsiveness to human situation around him,

Peace is not absence of conflict but the presence of creative alternative for responding to conflict- alternatives to passive or aggressive responses, alternatives to violence.

Dorothy Thompson-

because of the self-transcendence he has achieved, the self-expansion he has acquired. This is the growth of man from the stage of 'I' to 'I' and 'You' and further to 'We'. Hence spiritual growth of man manifests where man erects an expansive personality above his or her rigid individuality. It is then 'peace' sets in his heart and he radiates that 'peace' in the environment surrounding him. He develops capacity to make others peaceful. Other than the spiritual means, there are various theories expounded by different philosophies and scriptures, which prescribe for man, the righteous way of living so as to accomplish inner peace and tranquility.

According to the utilitarianism theory, which is the core of Indian philosophy, a person must act so as to bring about the greatest good of the greatest number of people possible.[7] Buddha prescribed the four noble truths concerning the sufferings of man; Dukha, Dukhasamudaya, Dukha- Nirodh, Dukha Nirodhak Marg and eight fold path as; Right Path, Right Resolve, Right Speech, Right Action, Right Living, Right Effort, Right Thought and Right Concentration. Similarly Jainism prescribed Samyag Darshan (right faith), Samyag Jnana (right knowledge) and Samyag Charitra (right conduct). The Bhagwat Gita mentions Bhakti, Jnana and Karma margas. Ancient Indian philosophers provided the concept of 'Purushartha'. Which explains the right way of living. Literally 'Purshartha' means what men live for? Central point of all these teachings is the righteous way of life a man should follow, not only for his/her peaceful existence but for all.

Jesus Christ assured, ' Kingdom of Heaven is Within Us'.[8] This implies that, we have to realise or experience this 'Heaven'

Peace has to be created, in order to be maintained. It is the product of faith, strength, Energy, Will, Sympathy, Justice, Imagination and the triumph of principle. It will never be achieved by passivity and quietism.

Dorothy Thompson-

by means of our own deeds. Peace is a divine asset and lasting emotion of human being, Srimad Bhagwat Gita assures (Chapter 2 and Chapter 16). 'Peace' can be accomplished by practicing certain values as: harmlessness (ahimsa), truth, absence of anger, renunciation(tyag), absence of crookedness, spirituality (vigour), forgiveness, patience, fortitude, purity, non-hatred (adroha), absence of over pride (abhiman) and absence of 'ego'. Fearlessness is foremost condition of human nature which is an important determinant of 'peace'. A man can achieve fearlessness by practicing detachment from his outer world (vairagya meva abhayam). Gita says, these are the virtues which all togther gives a complete picture of the nature of man of 'Divine Estate' (a man in complete peaceful state). Hence, 'peace' for individual is an inner state of mind and such a state of mind is not disturbed by external circumstances. An individual person having peaceful state of mind does not get affected by provocative behaviour of others and is beyond the pairs of opposites like good-evil, hot-cold and pleasure-displeasure. This type of individual is dispassionate but at the same time discharging his duties peacefully and diligently without expectation of reward. A person can cultivate peaceful mind by practicing 'Yoga', which is defined by Patanjali as 'stopping the modification of min' (Chitta Vritti Nirodha) These qualities or values are enumerated in Gita to serve as a living guide to all those who really want to accomplish inner peace or tranquility which is a 'Heaven' in Jesus words. The inner peace is a source of happiness in an individual, he is the only one who can spread happiness around and obverse is true as well. Happiness is a state of mind that is peaceful and contented and has less to do with changing external circumstances and more to do with our inner self.

J. Krishnamurti elaborates the idea of Peace in an individual context, because he believes that man himself is a

Inner peace is beyond victory or defeat.

Bhagavad-Gita -

world, he is the only source of 'peace' in the world. He explains the notion of peace in his book, 'Total Freedom' as ; 'Fear, pleasure, sorrow, thought of violence are all interrelated. Most of us take pleasure in violence, in disliking somebody, hating a particular race or group of people, having antagonistic feelings towards others. But in a state of mind in which all violence has come to an end there is a joy that is very different from the 'pleasure of violence."[9]

J. Krishnamurti describes Peace as a freedom from violence, an individual has to liberated from it only by looking in himself, "If we know how to look at violence, not only outwardly in society – the wars, the riots, the natioal antagonisms and class-conflicts but also in ourselves, then perhaps we shall be able to go beyond it."[10] He identifies the state of an individual when he is not in peace as;

"If you are free of violence in yourself the question is, "How to live in a world full of violence, acquisitiveness, greed, envy, brutality? Will I not be destroyed? When you ask such a question it seems to me you are not actually living peacefully?"[11]

According to J. Krishnamurti, everybody has violence in himself; he experiences violence in anger, violence in his sexual demands, violence in hatred, creating enemity and violence in jealousy. Violence is not merely killing another. It is violence when we use sharp words, when we make a gesture to brush away a person, when we obey because there is a fear. So violence is not merely organised butchery in the name of God, society or country. Violence is much more subtle, much deeper. Thus, to be free from violence, a man must expose himself to himself. He must try to understand violence not as an idea but as a fact

Peace begins with you.

J. Krishnamurti -

which exists in the human being. Only a liberated man, free from violence, is peaceful in this world.

A Vietnamese Zen Buddhist monk, Thich Nhat Hanh known as Thay says, 'if you want society to change, you have to change yourself. We tend to blame others for our sufferings. But don't forget that the other person is like that because you are like this, you are co-responsible, whether it is the Israel-Palestine. Hindu-Muslims, Catholic-Protestant, American-Arab situations of conflict or any other inter-personal antagonisms."[12]

The seers, monks or thinkers have attributed individuals to meaningful peace in the society, and hence in the world.

Acquisition of wealth and possessions do not pave the way to happiness. If it was true, why the U.S.A came down 23rd in the list of countries in recent 'Global Happiness Survey'.[13] Hence 'peace' is the pre-condition of happiness in an individual.

In individual context, peace is a subjective term and hence the 'happiness' too. Peace is an experience of inner calmness or tranquility which can be accomplished by practice. So, acquiring peace is an entirely individual effort and has less to do with external circumstances or external world. Even a wilderness or desert may be a paradise for a person having inner peace.

In the end, Rubaiyat of Omar Khayyam may be quoted,[14]
"Ah love could thou and I with fate conspire
To grasp this sorry state of things entire,
Would not be shatter it to bits and then
Re-mold it nearer to our hearts desire!"
A book of verses underneath the Bough
A jug of wine, a loaf of bread and Thou

Peace with in means peace with out

World peace Newletter-

Besides me singing in the wilderness,
Oh, wilderness were a paradise Enow.

Social Context

In social context, 'peace' implies the provisions of social justice and collective security to its citizens by a society. In any nation, societies have been formed and liable to maintain their social order on the basis of social justice. Thus 'peace' is perceived as the product of social justice. Hence, to conceptualise 'peace' in the social context, we have to look at the history of the idea of justice.

There is a long history of the development of the idea of justice. The idea or the concept of justice has always been different in different societies, but its concept has always been among the foremost concern to political theorists and philosophers. Plato was the first western philosopher who tried to develop the idea of justice. His 'Republic' is supposed to be a ten books long effort at defining justice in the state and in an individual.[15] According to Plato, "The nature of social justice could be discovered only by studying the harmony in that state. Hence, in general terms, Social Justice consists of the actions of individuals which the need of maintaining the social whole assigns them."[16]

In Christianity, justice was introduced as its subordination to charity and love and was differentiated from morality. Human Justice was distinguished from the divine justice.

After the liberating effects of renaissance, the idea of justice became secular or worldly. The idea of justice multiplied the worldly aspects of life, and affirmed a way of salvation

True peace is not merely the absence of tension: it is the presence of justice.

Martin Luther King J.R. -

through activities that were peculiarly human and mundane. But the secular consequences of 'renaissance' thoughts were not fully realised until 'the Natural Law' school of 16th and 17th centuries emerged. Rousseau was the main propagator of the 'Natural Law of Justice' But his idea of Natural Justice further took a distinctively anarchic turn in the social context. Kant defined Justice in the context of the society as : "Justice is the external liberty of each person limited by the liberty of all others."[17]

In the middle of the nineteenth century, Karl Marx the prophet of Socialism, the father of Communism and the practical philosopher as he was called, tried to study the political and economic problems and thus, to find the remedies for the world's ills. His mighty book, called 'Das Kapital' or 'Capital' influenced tremendously on the development of socialism in the world and became the Bible of Communist Russia. No thinker of the nineteenth century has such a direct, deliberate and powerful influence on mankind as Marx. He tried to offer the prospects of a perfect society in which there shall be no class distinction and every individual should get what he or she needs.

In the development of the idea of justice, at early stage Marx was influenced by Hegel's dialectics and Charles Darwin's Theory of Evolution. Further he developed his own Scientific Socialism and Humanism. Gradually Marxism became the 'dogma' and led the bloody struggles between bourgeois and proletariats in industrial societies.

At the end of nineteenth century, with the commencement of English Neo-liberalism, the concept of ' Human Rights' began to evolve and 'Social Justice' gradually took the position of 'Equality of Opportunity' and 'Minimum Standard of Living'. As idea of 'Human rights' emerged, the blend of justice and morality began to dilute. Thus, in the history of ideas, justice and morality were either identified, confused or too completely separated.

However 'justice' has been always supposed to be a prior condition and essential medium for the realisation of moral ideas. John Rawls in his book, 'A theory of Justice' has tried to clarify the issue of 'Social Justice' in the context of 'Equality of Opportunity'. He has put two principles: Principle of Liberty and Principle of Difference. He argues that all members of society are to have considerable and equal opportunities to gain any allowable position of favourable inequality, say wealth and power. He assumes that some inequality will indeed be required in any society, if all of its members are to be as well as they can be.[18]

Rawls' views about the position of an individual or community in society is in conformance with that of Plato. Overall inequality is necessary in maintaining the social harmony which is an indicator of Social Justice. But history of mankind reveals that, in social systems, initial advantages are sometimes magnified into comprehensive and highly stable systems of inequality, control and domination that employ the mighty force of custom, language, law, social structure, economic order, the state, the religion and prevailing technology to uphold inequalities. Perhaps the most familiar examples are slavery and subordination of women, by systems of dominance and severe inequalities that were institutionalised and enforced by the most powerful forces available. These included individual and collective terror and violence by the members of dominant groups provided by official and unofficial, law, custom and convention, social and economic structure, politicians, theological and religious organisation.[19] The Indian caste system is always quoted as relevant example of social exploitation and structural violence. Johan Goltung define 'peace' in this very context as, 'the absence of both direct, and structural violence."[20]

Generally western writers attack on the Indian caste system as it has been a mythical act of injustice and violence in the society. They are against the ongoing caste system in India, and ascribe it to poverty and all types of disparities in the Indian society. But at this stage, this must be clarified that the present caste system is the transformation of the ancient 'Varna' system which was based on Guna (Satva, Rajas, Tama) or nature of the people, who were free to manifest their nature for maintaining the harmony in the society. As Swami Vivekananda says, "This was the 'Varna System' which held the Indian society for three thousand years of its peaceful existence;" but he criticised the prevailing caste system from Brahmin period to downward history of Indian society as he addresses, "The masses who comprise the lowest caste through ages of constant tyranny of the higher caste, has totally lost their manliness and became like professional beggars".[21]

Our other great political leaders and social reformers like Mahatma Gandhi, Raja Ram mohan Roy, Tilak and Pandit Jawahar Lal Nehru tried to eradicate poverty and other social evils and came to resolve them in modern context.

Mahatma Gandhi implicated the philosophy of 'Isavasya Upanishad' in his thought for the accomplishment of just society in economic terms.

As "Isavasyamidam Sarvam, yat kinch jagatyam jagat'

Ten tyakten bhunjithah ma grdhah kasyasvit dhanam."

(states, the idea that wealth cannot be purely private possession and its accumulation should not be sole pursuit and that one should enjoy by sharing it with others)

When the power of love over comes the love of power the world will know peace.

Jimi Hendrix-

Gandhi developed this idea for application to the modern world of capital, land and labour. He said that property and wealth possessed or acquired by the haves should be deemed to be held in trust for benefits and welfare of all. A good and enlightened government itself could be a trust on a vast scale.[22]

The Gita says, that noble king like 'Janak' attained nobility by actions intended for 'Lok Sangrah' or people's welfare (Gita, III 20). After independence, Pandit Nehru formed the first government and tried to follow the path of democratic socialism to tackle the century old problems of India's poverty and backwardness.

Architects of Indian Constitution were very much influenced by the salient feature of the Universal Declaration of Human Rights (1948), therefore text of the Constitution embodied all those values and visions which are related to protection and promotion of fundamental rights of people and which are necessary and precondition of a peaceful and harmonious existence of society. In Indian Constitution, justice occupies the first place followed by liberty, equality, fraternity and unity of the nation.

Unfortunately the elements of our Constitution have not been incorporated seriously and honestly in our efforts to construct a just society and maintaining social order and harmony where every citizen could be secure. Constitutional provisions have been generally misinterpreted and misused by our politicians. Which consequently have led bloody clashes among people on the basis of caste, region, language, religion, sects and so on so forth.

The contrarieties in the concept of social justice and human rights have pushed the societies into unrests and agitations all over the world. It is difficult to define 'Peace' in a social context because the combination of social justice, human rights and morality is very difficult to operate in the societies. Thus conceptualisation of Peace in social context implies a fact that external conditions or reforms imposed on society for peace and harmony have not proved successful as history witnesses. Various kinds of socio-political systems like Capitalism, Socialism and Communism have not led to a peaceful society. Hence, seemingly, existence of a peaceful society can only depend on constituent members or individuals having peaceful minds; they are the only source of lasting peace in any society.

However, as an ideal Peace has always been conceptualised and defined in social context by the philosophers, social reformers and political thinkers in India and west alike. It is an ageless demand of any society.

International Context

'Peace' in international context can be perceived from two perspectives. One from the perspective of war and the other from the perspective of global trade.

Perspective of War

The idea of 'peace' in modern world has emerged in the context of the holocaust of two world wars which human society had witnessed. If a war is fought in any part of the world, it perverts human civilisation as a whole. At international level, militaristic thinking in different nations motivate them to use force or war in solving their disputes or conflict with other nations. Other than this, there is also a tendency among powerful and developed nations to prove their supremacy by attacking weaker nations (having weak military strength). Sometimes if nations have depositories of sophisticated and powerful weapons they are used to sell or supply those weapons to other nations to clear their stockpiles and thus encourage them to fight.

The creation of the nuclear bombs, the development of biological and chemical warfare and the manufacture of high-tech weaponry have elevated the danger of war and organised terrorism to a point where the future of mankind can no longer be taken for granted. Stockpiles of nuclear weapons in various Nuclear States and in the custody of terrorist group as Talibans backed by Al-Queda are big threat to the very existence of human civilisation.

Today, people are aware of the terrible destructive nature of the modern sophisticated weapons or Weapons of Mass Destruction (WMD) and hence they are frightened about whether or not there will be a future? Concern about the impending nuclear holocaust has generated need of 'Peace' in the world as whole. Thus, in the international context, much concern about 'peace' relates to nations and their ability to settle disagreements and conflicts without resorting to war. Internationally, peace implies that the government of nation states respect for the sovereignty of other nations and all nations of the world are going to use methods other than force or war to manage conflicts among them. Today, high-tech society has brought the human race to a point where it can no longer rely on militaristic ways to resolve differences but have to adopt non-violent solution of international problems and conflicts. Thus, in the international perspective, peace implies the development of a sense of the world as a global community where the citizens are required to have interest in the problems of people throughout the planet; have concern for social justice and human rights of all; have awareness of the war problems; have tolerance for racial and cultural differences; have unwillingness to use violence; have unselfishness and must have an attitude of globalism rather than patriotism. The people have awareness of the perplex condition of the planet earth and they must have respect for the ecological requirements of the earth.

Internationally, if people are concerned for the earth for the world wide human community and for the sacredness of life, there will be less support for the use of force or violence to settle disputes and disagreements. Consequently militarism and warfare in the world will be almost at end. It is said that, war is fought first in the minds of Generals. It shows the importance of mental attitude of persons in authority which can lead nations to war and destroy the global peace. So people should be careful in choosing their leaders to head their government, the leader whose attitude is towards reconciliation and not towards confrontation.

Earlier, Nationalism and Patriotism were recognised great virtues but now it is realised that such attributes of Nationalism and Patriotism create divisive tendency and people of one nationality become adversaries of other nationality. So, for global peace, we have to rise above narrow and parochial concepts of Nationalism and Patriotism and should embrace the whole universe in our thinking.

Perspective of Global Trade

Peace in the context of global trade can best be perceived by an example (based on the article of Shashi Tharoor, "Are North, South heading for a Cold War?). Today globalisation has surprisingly affected the international affairs in the world. The recent example is the running of Olympic Torch through countries for the Olympic Games organized by China. The running of Olympic Torch is meant to take the spirit of the games across the world engaging the public of some 48 countries. The Torch Relay was heavily protested and dogged openly in the northern world as in Paris, London, and San-Francisco for the cause of Tibetians. On the other hand, in southern world including India, public and protesters had been kept away from the relay in order to prevent aggressive protests by public over Chinese policies on Tibet. The torch run was a hollow exercise in upholding the dignity of China rather than the spirits of the Olympic.

In democracies like India and Buddhist nations as Srilanka and Thailand, the spiritual teachings of Dalai Lama have always found a far more universal appeal. His message of peace, love and reconciliation which could endure long after the recent crisis in Tibet has faded away from the headlines. For the sake of global trades and sovereignty of China, the principle of Human Rights and right to peaceful protests by people have been torn into shreds.

The response of Southern World to the recent crisis in Tibet is seen by some political analysts as an evidence of a more profound split in world affair between countries of the developing south actually conscious of China's sensitivities over its sovereignty and countries of the developed North outraged over Beijing's crackdown in Lhasa.

Although in the south, people have always been sympathetic with Tibetians by heart but the general tenor of both officials and media reaction have been respectful of China. In the recent chain of events, Pakistan and Nepal have been openly supportive of China while India kept silence over the matter. In this situation, a fear of Cold War between North and South could have exaggerated but this did not happen. The reason was that, South is aware of the behaviour of North. Northern-Western democracies are hypocratic in their behaviour. They preach about the need to respect Human Rights principles but their coddled military dictatorships in Asia had been unleashed when it suited them to do so from Pakistan to Philippines. The rest of the world see the preaching of North as tempered by self interest. Now the South is seemingly alert to any attempt by the world's Northern Colonial Powers to assert positions that undermine their hard-won and jealously safe guarded sovereignty. The southern countries are unlikely to grant unconditional loyality to the only Southern Superpower.

In the midst of all the very principles on which the world seems to be divided will continue to make headway amongst ordinary people across the world. But at the political and governmental levels fear of new Cold War is baseless. The great cause of the avoidance of new Cold War is the Global Trade.

As Shashi Tharoor says: " The need to tolerate differences and to bring the benefits of global trade to ordinary people everywhere, will continue to find adherents in both North and South."[23]

Hence global trade is the major cause, due to which, fears of a new cold war is unfounded and message of peace and love by Dalai Lama, a spiritual leader, a man of nonviolence is faded out from the headlines.

So, today how satirical is the concept of 'peace' in this context of global trade? This is not 'Peace'; it is just silence of common people maintained by their respective countries for the sake of present global trade.

A real global peace can be ensured, when global trade does not lead to exploitation of poor countries by 'rich', nor does it create imbalance in the world economy due to unethical practices. Maximisation of profit always hampers, the welfare of common people. Hence global-trade should endeavor to

We are not going to deal with the violence in our communities, our homes, and nation, until we learn to deal with the basic ethic of how we resolve our disputes and to place an emphasis on peace in the way we relate to one another.

Marian Wright Edelman-

maximising the happiness of people, rather than the maximum monetary profit. Thus, global trade, which is based on ethical values can only establish global peace.

However, after analysing the concept of peace in various contexts, a comprehensive definition of 'Peace' may be,

"Peace is well defined as a state of existence where neither the overt violence of war, nor the covert violence of unjust systems is used as an instrument for extending the interest of a particular nation or group. It is the world where basic needs are met and in which justice can be obtained and conflict resolved through non-violent process and human and material sources are shared for the benefit of all people." [24]

Mahatma Gandhi's Concept of Peace

Mahatma Gandhi was a great proponent of Peace in the world. He was a practical idealist. He interweaved the two cords of human knowledge and dynamics in life. His vision was holistic, hence he defined Peace from holistic point of view. His conception of Peace evolves in the context of violence. Contrary to violence there is non- violence which is producer of 'Peace', but he admitted that " Nobody can practice perfect non-violence. We may not be perfect in our use of it, but we definitely discard the use of violence" (Thomas Merton).[25] Non- violence practice does not just involve using Civil Disobedience or Asahayog against oppressors but demands a rigorous discipline where an individual orients his or her life towards working harmoniously with others. Non-violence implies taking an active stance in the world to manage conflicts constructively and to work for peace and justice. Gandhi was in favour of non-violence and

Non- cooperation is a measure of discipline and sacrifies and it demands respect for the opposite views.

Mohan das K. Gandhi -

more civilised life style. In his view, violence means : exploitation which a nation practices with other nation, a society practices with other society, a system practices on another system and an individual practices on another individual. Exploitation is a cause of unrest and insecurity among people. A nation or society can live in peace and harmony if, and only if there is security.

Modern weapons and technology are leading to a widening net of insecurity among peoples and nations alike. Weapons can not provide security, it is the morals and faith in God and Truth that leads to real sense of security.[26]

In the period of globalisation, Gandhian concept of security can provide a great sense of strength and confidence among people of the world. Today great changes are occurring in the world due to modern technology. "Change is the law of nature", is a universally accepted fact. Change involves innovations and zest for life, hence the ultimate end of technology should be security, prosperity, development and peace. Unfortunately besides material development, it is not happening. So humanity has to explore for the ageless human need of a permanent security.

Today, there are recurring experiences of innovations in the sector of Mass Destruction through terror, mishaps and cold blooded and planned assaults against humanity at large. Present day global needs and diverse scenario of weapons of mass destruction, depletion of resources, pollutions, terrorism, immorality in modern civil society, mutual suspicions, among people and nations alike appear to be self defeating.[27] Gandhian concept of 'Peace' and Non-Violence emerge from individuals and extends vis-à-vis states to broader global perspectives.

If you want to make peace, you don't talk to your friends. You talk to your enemies.

Moshe Dayan-

Gandhian views and visions are still alive in the world with holistic perception of truth, foresightedness and scientific analysis of the conflicts and violence in the human society.

Gandhi sees security from different aspects of a civil society as: individuals, groups, administrative units, police forces, provinces, sovereignty of states or nations, international and global organisations. Gandhian thought about 'peace' revolves around the intrinsic relationships between knowledge and wisdom on one hand, and the security of a civil society comprising the connections amongst these aspects from the level of an individual to an international establishment and global order, on the other. Security, defence and peace have to begin with the individual first and other levels of security will have to follow the suit.

This is the Gandhian prescription for the development of security and peace in the world.

Gandhian view of security and peace for both an individual and state can be meaningful only if certain interrelated measures are taken by the world community. These measures are.

- Global conventional and nuclear disarmament.
- Preservation of environment and ecology.
- Resolving the population, poverty and unemployment problems.
- Thinking more of peace than about war and weapons.
- Globalisation with a human face.
- Evolving a world culture where smallest should feel the tallest.[28]

Hence, in nutshell, Gandhian theory of 'Peace' acclaims human values. For Mahatma Gandhi, Nonviolence (Ahimsa) is a way of life rather than a tactics or strategy. When non-violence combine together with the search for truth (Satyagrah) it makes difference between passive submission to injustice and an active struggle against it. The struggle for justice excludes both physical violence and casting the opponent in the role of enemy and hence presupposes compassion and self criticism. Gandhian notion of Welfare to All (Sarvodaya) recognises 'Peace' as incompatible with exploitation or inequality of wealth.[29]

In economic terms, Gandhi implicates the idea of Isavasya Upanishad for the modern world of capital, land and labour. According to him, one should enjoy wealth by sharing it with others.

Gandhi does not take 'Peace' as an end, but a continuous revolutionary process, where ends cannot be separated from means.

References

1. Harris Ian, M, (1988). *Peace Education* London, Mc Farland and Company, Inc. Publication.

2. Galtung, J. (1969) Violence, Peace and Peace Research. *Journal of Peace Research, 6.*

3. Ranganathananda (1986).*Eternal Values for a Changing Society,* Bombay, Bhartiya Vidya Bhavan, p. 107.

4. Grewal, S (2004). Education for Peace: Concept and Need, *On Education for Peace Our Main Priority.* Ludhiyana, Malwa College of Education for women.

5. Harris, op. cit, p.7.

6. Ranganathananda, op. cit., pp. 180-182.

7. Pandeya, A.N. (1992). Social Justice, *Education in Values.* New Delhi, NCERT.

8. Ranganathananda. op. cit., p. 257.

9. Krishnamurti, J. Freedom from Violence is True Liberation, Excerpt from *Total Freedom,* The Times of India 2009, Jan, 25.

10. *Ibid.*

11. *Ibid.*

12. Ganesh, N (2008), Pilgrimage to Peace, Times of India, Nov. 4.

13. The *(un)* Happy Planet Index (2006) An Index of human well being and environmental impact. ne.f (new economic foundation) Friends of Earth. http://en. wikipedia. org/wiki/Happy Planet-Index.

14. Fitz. Gerald, E. *Rubaiyat of Omar Khayyam* (translation), 5th Ed., Verse XII, p. 156.

15. Mc. Bride, W.L. (1975). *The Concept of Justice in Marx, Engels and others,* Ethics. Chicago, The University of Chicago Press, 85.

16. Upadhyay, P. (2005). Spirits of Human Rights and Poverty: Holistic Perspective, S.N. Chaudhary (ed), *Human Rights and Poverty in India: Theoretical Issues and Empirical Evidences,* New Delhi, Concept Publishing Company, p. 100.

17. *Ibid.*, pp. 100-101.

18. Rawl, J. (1971). *A Theory of Justice* Cambridge, Mass.

19. Upadhyay, op. cit. p. 103.

20. Sorensen, Georg. (1992). Utopianism in Peace Research, The Gandhian Heritage. *Journal of peace Research*, Vol. 29, No-3

SAGE PUBLICATION, on line. http//Jpr. sagepub.com/egi/content/abstract

21. Upadhyay, op. cit., p. 105.

22. Chaudhary, T.N. (1991). Gita- The Light Universal, *Bhavan Journal* Vol. 57. No. 21 Bombay, Bhartiya Vidya Bhavan.

23. Tharoor, S. (2008). Are north, south leading for a cold war? Shashi on Sunday The Times of India, April 27.

24. Harris, op. cit., p. 7.

25. Merton, T. (1964).*Gandhi on Non-Violence* New York, New Directions.

26. Gangal, A. (2008). Quest for Harmony in an Age of Globalisation and Weapons of Mass Destruction. http//www/scribd. com/doc/Gandhi-concept Human-Security http//www.the freelibrary.com/Mahatma+Gandh+Concepts+ of+Global+Security+And+Peace.

27. *Ibid.*

28. *Ibid.*

29. Bose, Anima (1981). A Gandhian Perspective on Peace, *Journal of peace Research* Vol. 18, No. 2 159-164, SAGE Journal on line. httpp//jpr.sage pub.com/cgd/content/abstract

3

Approaches to Peace

The contextual analysis of the concept of 'Peace reveals that, 'Peace', as a state of mind of an individual, as harmony in the society and as peaceful existence of a nation and the world, cannot be fully accomplished; it can only be approached by some means. That is why, Mahatma Gandhi recognised peace as not an end but a continuous revolutionary process where ends can be separated from means. Since the concept of 'Peace is contextual, hence is the approach to peace. Different strategies are used in different contexts or circumstances to approach peace.

In times of war, approach to peace indicates certain actions to stop war or terminate the violence. If it is not possible to cease war then the strategy for peace is to increase defence measures and militaries to fight against hostile enemy state. To stop war and settle down the conflicts and disagreements among the nation states, there is also an approach that, to build

They have not wanted peace at all; they have wanted to be spared war——— as though the absence of war was the same as peace.

Dorothy Thompson-

up international organisations, effective enough to control war and protect the human society from terror and holocaust of world war. The building of League of Nations and United Nations Organizations were such approaches to accomplish peace in the world after two world wars.

In the social context to maintain peace and harmony in the society, the approach is, to provide social justice and collective security to its citizens. Hence, to maintain peace in the society, poor and oppressed class or the masses should be released from their prevailing miserable and pathetic conditions by the provisions by satisfying their basic needs, by educating them, by providing them with equal opportunities for development and protecting their rights by the laws and constitutions of the nation.

In the context of everyday social life, to stop the violence and secure the lives of citizens, the approach to peace is to punish antisocial, violent, murderous and roguish people by implementing the law. Society is made secure by strengthening the judiciary and courts (the apex bodies of justice).

In the context of the individuals in the society, means of attaining peace of mind or inner peace is to create spiritual and moral strength in oneself. The scriptures of all religions say that, an individual is the ultimate source of peace in the world. When J. Kirshnamurti says, ***"You are the world. You are the human being that has made this world of utter disorder, the world that is crying helplessly in great sorrow, it is you, the human being that has built the world. So the world outside is not different from the world in which you live***

One is left with the horrible feeling now that war settles nothing; that to win a war is as disastrous as to lose one.

Unknown-

your private life,"[1] he wants to express that, every individual or human being has to be changed to change the outer world, because he is who, that has created this world. This is possible only by educating the minds of human beings or individuals. Hence, educating minds of individuals is now considered the last approach or strategy to develop peace in this world. This is why the first statement in the Preamble of the Constitution of UNESCO is; ***"Since war begins in the minds of men, it is the minds of men that the defence of peace must be constructed."***[2] Thus education for peace is founded in UNESCO'S constitutional mandate to build peace in the minds of men.

Further, various approaches to peace are dealt elaborately in the text so as to make people aware of the peace strategies. Some people with specific bend of mind think that balance of power or peace through strength is the only approach to create and maintain peace in the world.

Balance of Power

At the international level, it is believed that 'peace' in the world can be accomplished and maintained only by the 'balance of power'. The balance of power means, approximate equality of defense measures or military forces of the countries.

If a country is superior to the other with respect to its military force and war weapons, the weak country feels threatened and insecure. Consequently, the weaker country starts strengthening its defensive power to make secure its territories, sovereignty and its citizens. To strengthen the defensive power, the developing countries of the world are increasing their budgets for the defence and militaries.

In peace the sons bury their fathers, but in war the fathers bury their sons.

Croesus-

Generally, countries have fear of catastrophic consequences of going to war, so they proceed towards massive armaments to make the balance of power.

In modern terms, 'peace' through balance of power involves, nuclear deterrence. Today, super powers of the world are emphasising on 'nuclear deterrence' so as to discourage developing countries in proceeding towards nuclear arms. The balance of power is also called 'peace through strength', but this approach to global peace enforces the value of militarism in the societies which obviously influence the political, social, economic and cultural ethos of the nations.

Peace through strength is an idea which is the outcome of the belief that war and violence are the only legitimate ways to manage human affairs in the society. There is a belief of Roman Empire, ***"If you desire peace, prepare for war."***[3] This is very strange to know that the first world war was fought to end the war and to make the world safe for democracy and peace.

Now the balance of power as a strategy to maintain peace in the world is being criticised in many ways by economists and sociologists throughout the world because the expenditure on military and war weapons has been increased recklessly not by some countries only rather by the world as a whole. This expenditure has exceeded by the large proportion of the total expenditure on education, health care and other important services throughout the world. This tendency has absorbed the creativity and talents of more than millions of research specialists and engineers and has ruined the talents of those who are capable of providing more civilised and effective

We make war that we may live in peace.

Aristotle-

strategies to resolve the conflicts and disagreements among the nations.

The strategy, 'peace through strength' is strengthened not only at the international level but at the community and individual levels also. Presently in the society groups of people and individuals are inclined to possess arms for self defense. Increasing insecurity due to terrorism and failing law and order in day to day life of society, people are proceeding to own arms for their own security and peace. This tendency is indisputably disquieting in itself but what is more disturbing still, is the fact that this is a trend which is becoming increasingly strengthened. This trend has created many types of psychosocial problems in the society.

Furthermore, the whole world is involved in the arms-race. On one hand, super powers are addressing for nuclear deterrence and on the other, they are clearing the stockpiles of nuclear weapons unused. They provoke the weaker developing or under developed countries to fight so that they could supply arms to them and clear their depositories.

Presently, a big part of sophisticated arms and nuclear weapons is smuggled across the countries by terrorist groups to make disasters and to destroy the peace of people and the nations. It is the irony of modern civilisation that, the nuclear power which was invented for human welfare, has become the Weapon of Mass Destruction (WMD) and a tool of destruction of not only of world peace but also of large scale destruction of eco-system of the planet earth.

Today, human society at large is feeling insecure in this world where available stockpiles of weapons are providing a peculiar sense of security with threats of complete human extinction. This approach to security and peace is strange and ironical. Without security, no 'peace' is possible and modern sense of security in the world is possible only through mutual assured destruction (MAD). What a dilemma it is ?

The balance of power or peace through strength is the strategy which is the outcome of peculiar type of thinking which needs transformation for the sake of peoples peace in this world.

Establishment of Institutions

After the First World War, League of Nations was established in 1920 so as to further terminate violence and war from the world, but it did not happen. World War II was fought in 1939-45. The people of the world experienced the catastrophe of two world wars. Consequently they came forward to establish legal and political international institutions with the hope that, they would play an effective role in the termination of wars and in the peaceful resolution of conflicts among the nations at international level, This was the reason, why United Nations Organisation was created in 1942. The charter of United Nations provides measures for the prevention of war and relief from the threats to peace in the world.

The UNESCO, an agency of United Nations Organisation was established to promote peace and security among nations of the world by developing collaborations in the field of education, science and culture. The UNESCO, has also promoted the affirmations enumerated in the Charter of the UN for the peoples of the world, without distinction of race, sex, language and religions. The purpose of UNESCO is to further universal respect for justice, for the rule of the law, for the human rights and fundamental freedom in the World.

Now more and more international laws and institutions are being created to resolve conflicts, disagreements and to

There never was a good war or a bad peace.

Benjamin Franklin

control the wars among the nations and to promote peace. Critics of this strategy indicate its limitations as generally there are some countries who are inclined to fight with other countries to resolve their disagreements or disputes; and there are some who go for war just to prove their supremacy over the others. The nation state having such type of policies, do not have interest in other peaceful means to resolve their problems. They don't believe on arbitration to resolve their disputes; they enjoy fighting to impose their will on the other nations. In this case, the international institutions become ineffective because there is no effective non-military way to punish such countries who violate international laws and treaties.

Today, people of the world feel insecure to see the helplessness and ineffectiveness of these apex international institutions of the world. The recent examples are: invasions by America, on Iraq, terrorists attack 9/11 on World Trade Centre, New York in America and consequent attack on Afghanistan by it as 'War on terror', continuous historical conflicts and fights in middle east countries; Israel, Palestine and Lebanan, strained relations between India and Pakistan due to Pakistan supported terrorism in India and increasing tendencies of Wars among Islamic and non-Islamic countries. These are the examples which show the helplessness of United Nations Security Council in protecting the blood-feuding people and kids of these countries from outrages of world powers and terrorist organisations. UN is already struggling with its role of peace keeping by mediation and conflict resolution in this volcanised world, and hence this is the great source of insecurity and fear among the people.

The poor long for riches, the rich long for heaven, but the wise long for a state of tranquility.

Swami Rama-

Peace Through Ethical and Moral Strength

All religions, saints and seers, and holy scriptures of the world have prescribed ethical and moral values to induce and maintain peace in an individual and in the society by and large.

As far as India is concerned, it has always stood for peace through ethical and moral strength. This strength evolves through dharma (religion). Here dharma is not a sectarian concepts rather it is social ethics which treat a man as a member of a social group. Social ethics direct the conduct of man interacting with the external social environment, enriching it economically, politically and culturally and hence he himself in turn gets enriched in character, efficiency, political awareness and social and human concerns.

Ethical values find manifestation in the context of interaction among human beings and society. Ethics is therefore inseparable from social context and vice-versa. It is the cementing factor uniting man with man in the Society. Ethical values are implied expressions of dharma. Dharma has two aspects- one is 'abhyudaya' or social welfare, the other aspect is 'nihsreyasa' or trans-social spiritual dimension or spiritual liberation.

In Mahabharata, dharma is defined as abhyudaya as that which hold together, that which sustain all human beings.

धारणात् धर्मन् इत्याहुः
धर्म धारयति प्रजाः ।

dharnat dharman ityayuh
dharm dharayati prajah

Hence 'dharma' in India implies social welfare and spiritual liberation for peaceful existence and sustenance of human society.

In 'Manu Smriti' dharma is explained as the manifestation of ten moral values;

घृतिः क्षमा दमोस्तेयम शौचम् इंदियनिग्रहः।
धीः विद्या सत्यम् अक्रोधः दशकम् धर्म लक्षणः।।

dhritih ksamâ damo asteyam
saucam indriya nigrahah
dheeha vidya satyam akrodhah
dasakam dharma laksanah.

fortitude or patience, forgiveness, control on desires, abstention from theft internal and external purity or hygiene, control of senses, wisdom, knowledge, truthfulness, absence of anger, quietude are ten virtues or qualities, which should be manifested through 'dharma'

The Bhagwad Gita in Chapter –16, stanza 1-3 emphasises the cultivation of certain virtues in people so as to achieve 'Divine Estate', ie 'Peace'. Twenty six values, enumerated in these verses are as follows:

अभयं सत्वसंशुद्धिर्ज्ञान योगव्यवस्थितः।
दानं दमश्च यज्ञश्च स्वाध्यायस्तप आर्जवम ।।1।।

abhayam sattvasam suddhir
Jnanayogavyavasthitih
danam damas ca yajans ca
svadhyayas tapa arjavam.

Moreover:

अहिंसा सत्यमक्रोधस्त्यागः शान्तिरपैशुनम!।
दया भूतेष्वलोलुहवं मार्दवं ह्रीरचापलम!।। 2।।

ahinsa satyam akrodhas
tyâgas sântir apaisunam

daya bhutesv aloluptam
mardavam hrir acapalam

Moreover:

तेज क्षमा घृतिः शौचमद्रोहो नातिमानिता।
भवन्ति संपद दैवीममिजातस्य भारत।। 3।।

tajah ksamâ dhritih sâucam
adroho na timanita
bhâvanti sampadam daivim
abhijatasya bhârata

A man can live a noble way of life by accepting and living these aforementioned values of life while meeting his day to day world.

Fearlessness (abhayam) comes first. Lord Krishna, a divine Acharya, indicates that true ehtical perfection in one is directly proportional to the spiritual unfoldment attained by the individual. The other virtues which are the core of all moral living are purity of heart, knowledge and Yoga, alms-giving, control of the senses, sacrifice, study of sastras, austerity, straight forwardness, harmlessness or non-violence (Ahimsa), truth, absence of anger, renunciation, absence of crookedness, compassion, un-covetousness, gentleness, modesty, absence of fickleness, vigour, forgiveness, fortitude, purity, absence of hatred, absence of over pride and ultimate value i.e. 'Peace' These qualities are enumerated to serve as a living guide to all those who want to live in peace. In the perspective of all these values, we can recognise our way of life and change our vision of the world around us on the above lines, to that extent we shall economise our energies, that are often wasted in idle pursuits. To respect and live these values of life completely is to assure ourselves of the right way of living and hence a peaceful existence. The Gita has prescribed three noble paths or margas, Karma, Bhakti and Jnana for the people of different temperaments in the world to attain spiritual liberation or 'Mukti', so as to attain, 'a lasting peace'.

The concept of 'purushartha' points out the four supreme ends, arth (wealth), kama (physical well-being), dharma (righteousness) and moksha (spiritual liberation), which one should get in accordance with dharma.

There exist many more examples in Indian scriptures and philosophies which may throw further light on the nature and conception of ethical and moral values in view of their special relevance to the modern context in dealing with challenges of modern life.

Mahatma Buddha prescribed four noble truths concerning sufferings of human beings Dukha, Dukhasamudaya, Dukhanirodha, Dukh nirodhaka marg and eight fold paths as; right path, right resolve, right speech, right action, right living, right effort, right thought and right concentration to attain lasting peace. Similarly,Jainism's prescription of Samyag darshan (right faith) Samyag Jnan (right knowledge) and Samyag charitra (right conduct) are the noble means to attain peaceful and harmonious living. Not only in India but in other religions and philosophies of the world, ethical values find manifestation in the context of interaction between man and society. Thus, they find expression in an as outward movement of love and concern for the others. This is well expressed in the great utterance of Jesus Christ; ***"Love Thy Neighbour as Thy self".*** The great philosopher Kant said, ***"Two things fill me with wonders, starry heaven above and moral laws within."***[4]

We look forward to the time when the Power of love will replace the Love of Power. Then will our world know the blessing of peace.

William E. Gladstone-

Hence love and concern for others and moral laws are the basic factors for the induction of peace in an individual and in the society by and large.

From Western point of view, the word morality comes from the Latin root 'moralis' or "customs" and quite simply is defined as the "principles of behaviour in accordance with standards of right or wrong." If an individual wants to live morally, who will decide the standards of right or wrong is a question on which Theosophical literature is ambivalent.

Madame Blavatsky in 'Practical Occultism says that, ***"meditation, abstinence, the observation of moral duties, gentle thoughts, good deeds and kind words .... are the most efficacious means for obtaining knowledge and preparing for reception of higher wisdom."***[5] Further, a theosophist Henry Olcott saw morality as closely linked to the outcomes of karma. He says in Buddhist Occultism that ***"Karma is a causation operating on the morals. Buddhism believe that there is no miracle in human affairs; what a man sows that he must and will reap."***[6]

Critics of this strategy find the concept of morality confusing because there is not a clear description of what moral standards ought to be. The standards of morality are always very difficult to define. Moral values vary in time and place for different cultures and social groups. For most people moral values are closely tied to conventions offered by the societies in which they live. The standards of right or wrong in various societies and in various times are conflicting. So moral living is

Religion and science both profess peace (and the sincerity of the professors is not being doubted), but each always turns out to have a dominant part in any war that is going or contemplated.

Howard Nemerov:-

very difficult in the fast changing scenario of global framework. Specially when the world is standing at the threshold of major social transformation and is in the grip of terror and violence, most people find the old moral and ethical values inadequate and irrelevant in providing them strength and fullfilling their material needs. This approach has failed in solving the problems of physical ailments of man and his material poverty and distress. Not only this, people who want to live moral life in the present chaotic and violent world, are entangled in moral conflicts. The situation is disquieting and disturbing for a man who wants to live morally a peaceful life.

On the contrary, most of the people are in favour of peace through ethical and moral strength in the individual self because this is the only approach which can provide them strength to survive amidst the materially affluent, chaotic and brute world. They find the material development and achievements of modern civilization which rely on physical science and technology, inadequate and partial. They opine that, science and technology are helpless today to solve the problems of mental ailments, distress and inner poverty of modern man in the midst of external material affluences. Einstein had confessed; ***"Physical science can denature plutonium, but it can not denature evils in*** the heart of man."[7]

The modern material development can sharpen the organic appetite of man and provide him with ever increasing range and quantity of consumer goods and gadgets to satisfy that appetite, but it can not offer concrete help to man, to check his impulses to indulge in lust and greed, drink and drugs, violence, and destruction and even suicide. These are the human unfullfillment today individually and collectively. These are the basic sources of human miseries of modern life. Today man has lost his natural spiritual strength. Amidst the world of money, wealth, market, intellectual properties, man has become poor inwardly. This is the spiritual poverty. Today people understand well only the strength arising from the energy resources of money, of muscle, and of brain, but very few are realising that, all these types of strengths will be washed away by even a small temptation of sex and money. Sri Ramkrishna Paramhansa expressed it – ***"Whereas, spiritual strength will hold a man steady against waves and waves of all such temptations...... A tree that is rooted firm in the soil will stand steady against all the winds that blow, but a lightly rooted tree will fall down even by a gentle breeze. Jesus says: A house built on rocks will stand, ... one built on sand collapses easily.***[8] Hence there is no way other than, to deal all the temptations through the means of moral and spiritual strength.

This is a crucial period of social transformation and psycho-social evolution, as it is said. Hence it is believed that, all those ethical and moral values pertaining to old conventions are not relevant and operational in the present context. If this is the situation man has to turn towards the avenue of those core values which are still relevant and helpful in the modern perspective of fast changing world.

Now presently, people throughout the world are exploring the science of spirituality. Today most people believe that for the knowledge and technical know how of dealing with the sources of inner discord of modern man and the society, man has to turn towards the science of spirituality.[9] This can be proved to be strength and the only way, that can provide modern man with that science of human possibilities to help and guide the long course of psycho-social evolution a modern man is facing. In this connection, Sri Sri Ravi Shanker says; ***"spiritual aids can help one pull back from the brink of chaos and restore the balance and oneness. When you are spiritual, nothing can shake you, spirituality gives you a lot of strength."***[10] Hence Spirituality seems to be the key for peaceful existence of man and ultimately the society. Through the science of spirituality, people of every religion and faith may discover the truth of their own faith through their own experiences and that will create true harmony ultimately.[11] Through the journey of spiritual awakening man may certainly develop some fundamental values which are the necessary condition for inner peace in an individual and harmony in the society.

In fact, new age spiritual leaders are furthering the thought that all religions basically preach the same ethical values or code of conduct – love, compassion, selflessness, forgiveness, oneness and service of others.

The Bible puts it thus: ***"God is love, and he that dwelleth in love, dwelleth in God and God in him."***[12]

Islam advises: *The poor the orphan and the captive – feed (them) for the love of God, for the sake of Him alone, desiring no reward, not even thanks.*[13]

Hence, love and concern for others is the core of integration in any society. In Bible, Jesus Christ says; "Love thy neighbour as thy self". This does not mean, 'love' for physical neighbour rather it is the love and concern for the whole.

Carl Sagan, the well-known astronomer, in his book 'Cosmos' writes that

"Human history can be viewed as a slowly dawning awareness that we are members of a large group .... If we are to survive, our loyalties must be broadened further to include the whole humanity, the entire planet earth."[14]

First keep the peace with in yourself, then you can also bring peace to others.

Thomas A Kempis:-

J. Krishnamurti also warned: ***"A materialistic humanity will destroy itself unless the self is wholly abandoned."***[15] The abandonment of self is love, compassion for all things the starving, the suffering, the homeless and even for the materialist.

It is the individual who makes the world and therefore it is each individual's loving, caring thought, feeling and action which help in transforming the world. Hence, to approach peace in this world, 'Love for all' is the most powerful of all moral and ethical values. This is the concretisation of spirituality in human behaviour. Only a spiritual person can transmit love to all and radiate peace in the world surrounding him. Spirituality makes man liberated and free from violence. According to J. Krishnamurti, 'freedom from violence' is peace. If we want a peaceful life, we have to get rid of violence. How can it be done, he explains lucidly in his book, 'Total Freedom', "We could go to the very root of violence and be free from it, otherwise we might live forever in battle with each other. If that is the way you want to live – and apparently most people do – then carry on; if you say, 'Well I'm sorry, violence can never end. Then you and I have no means of communications, you have blocked yourself; but if you say there might be a different way of living, then we shall be able to communicate with each other."

So let us consider together, those of us who can communicate, whether it is at all possible totally to end every form of violence in ourselves and still live in this brutal world. I think it is possible. I don't want to have a breath of hate, jealousy, anxiety or fear in me.

If we know how to look at violence, not only outwardly in society – the wars, the riots, the national antagonism and class conflicts but also in ourselves, then perhaps we shall be able to go beyond it.....

We are trying to understand violence not as an idea, but as a fact which exists in the human being, in myself. And to go into the problem I must be vulnerable, open, to it. I must expose myself to myself - not necessarily expose myself to you because you may not be interested – but I must be in a state of mind that demands to see this thing right to the end.

J. Krishnamurty explains that "every human being has violence in his inner self, only he is required to understand, I am a violent human being. This is obvious I have experienced violence in anger, violence in my sexual demands, violence in hatred, creating enmity and violence in jealousy. Violence is not merely killing another. It is violence when we use a sharp word, when we make a gesture to brush away a person, when we obey because there is fear. So violence is not merely organied butchery in the name of God, society, or country. Violence is much more subtle, much deeper and we are inquiring into the very depths of violence". ***When you call yourself an Indian, Muslim, Christian, European or anything else, you are being violent. Because you are separating yourself by belief, nationality or tradition, it breeds violence. So a man who is seeking to understand violence does not belong to any country, religion, political party or partial system; he is concerned with the total understanding of mankind."***[16]

Thus, the idea of J. Krishnamurti to approach peace is entirely individual endeavour; first to understand violence in his deeper self and next to get liberated from it. Freedom from violence is possible only by the science of spirituality. Though the growth of spirituality in the society, is necessarily a slow process, the concretion of spirituality is very difficult, for it means unlearning many old ways and means to tackle life, and learning many new ones. But the process should be started, so as to learn the core values of life in response to the growing challenges and situations in the present world, otherwise we are going to write our own epitaph.

Another great approach which is being tried out to terminate war and violence from the world and maintaining peace is pacifism.

Pacifism

Pacifism is an approach to peace which is based on belief that war and violence are morally unjustified and that all disputes should be settled by peaceful means. Under this approach, "Peace" comes from setting a peaceful example and avoiding physical violence to settle disagreements. Pacifists believe in non-violence. For them all forms of life are sacred, killing any form of life is immoral. They employ non-violent strategies to resolve conflicts and to deal human affairs.

Internationally, the approach of pacifism suggests disarmament of all the nations. According to Pacifists, to attain peace in the world, the nations should adopt non-violent measures as a means to counteract hostile invasions. They believe that, with disarmament of the nations, the threat of war would be greatly reduced.

All great religions of the world have shown the path of Pacifism, that is the path to promote moral and spiritual strength among the members of human society to counteract the challenges and all form of conflicts in the human world.

There are several examples of pacifists in the west as the early Christians who opposed conscriptions in the Roman army, Quakers in England in 17th century resisted; Cromwell's forced conscription in the British country sides. Not only this, there were groups of women who established Women International

He who lives in harmony with himself lives in harmony with the world.

Marcus Aurelius-

League for Peace and Freedom during the first Word War in Hague. The women of Greenham Common in Wales protested against government policy to install the cruise missile in all of the 102 NATO basis in Britain. In Japan, a group of Shibakusa women have built a permanent cottage in the foot of Mount Fizi to maintain permanent peace and protest camp. These examples show, how women groups have been stuggling to protest against war and violence. They are named Quakers who believe in Pacifism. However Pacifists in the world have mobilised support for alternatives to physical forces by using Civil Disobedience tactics. Mahatma Gandhi and Bertrand Russell are the great thinkers and socio-political activists of modern world, who propagated the non-violence means to resolve disagreements and dispute among the nations. They were labeled as pacifists.

Prof Bertrand Russel was fellow in Trinity College, Cambridge University. He was not only an honoured citizen of England but the recipient of several awards like, Order of Merit, Nobel Prize, Kalinga Prize, Jerusalem Prize, and so forth. Russell resisted specific wars, protesting them in specific ways, on the grounds that they were contrary to the interest of civilization and thus immoral. Russell's activism against British participation in World WarI led to fines, a loss of freedom of travel within Britain and the non-renewal of his fellowship at Cambridge University. He was eventually sentenced to prison in 1918 on the tenuous grounds that he had interfered in British Foreign Policy.

Russell used to spend his time in 1950s and 1960s for various political causes, primarily related to nuclear disarmament and opposing the Vietnam War. (Russell Vietnan War Crimes Tribunal). The Russell-Einstein Manifesto was a document calling for nuclear disarmament and was signed by eleven of the prominent nuclear physicists and intellectuals of the time.

In 1958, Russell became the first president of the 'Campaign for Nuclear Disarmament.' In 1961 he was imprisoned for a week for inciting Civil Disobedience when he took part in a huge ban-the-bomb demonstration at the Ministry of Defence, but the sentence was quashed on account of his age.

In 1963, he became the recipient of the Jerusalem Prize, an award for the writers concerned with the freedom of the individual in the society.

During the Cuban Missile Crisis, Russell sent telegrams to Kennedy, Khrushchev, the UN Secretary General U Thant, and British Prime Minister Macmillan to prevent further escalation and a possible nuclear war.

In 1963, the Bertrand Russell Peace Foundation began to work in order to carry forward Russell's work for peace, human rights and social justice. Russell along with the Jean-Paul Sartre organised a Tribunal what he called an International War Crimes Tribunal.

In this way political and social activism occupied much of Russell's time for most of his long life. He remained active politically to almost the end of his life, writing and exhorting world leaders and lending his name to various causes, specially non-violence and nuclear disarmament for world peace.[17]

The other great pacifist in the modern world was Mahatma Gandhi. In his autobiography 'The Story of My Experiments with Truth', Gandhi considered that truth in this world can not be discovered except through non-violence. There will always be conflicts, great and small, in human affairs. The nuclear bomb has made it obvious that total war can no longer settle conflicts. And clearly, no conflict can be ended in its inner reality by the alleged deterrence from the possession of nuclear weapons.[18]

Gandhi's struggle for the freedom of India was an example, where he showed that unity in people can be aroused fruitfully and enduringly by love and the desire for justice leading to the resolution of conflicts.

Gandhi propagated the theory of truth and non-violence in the world and he himself applied the theory in his day to day life. He believed that nonviolent means, based on the eternal law of 'love' is the single largest tool for resolving conflicts. According to him, nonviolence is not merely a personal virtue, it is also a social virtue, to be largely cultivated like other virtues. Nonviolence is always superior to violence. A society can be regulated through the means of non-violence in its mutual dealings of human affairs.

Gandhi believed that means are related to the end, violence can only produce counter violence. He showed by his practical experiences, several times in his life, that violence can be countered by nonviolence.[19]

Mahatma Gandhi had faith in the power of non-violence, that is why he trained people in this power and utilised it to foster the principle of nonviolence in bringing about India's freedom without bloodshed. Non-Cooperation and Satyagrah were the main practical tools to counter the repressive policies of British Raj. Richard B. Gregg in his book 'The Power of Non-violence' has shown more examples of nonviolent resistence in different countries and at different times. He has quoted few outstanding examples, where non violence resistance was used by individuals in some instances and in other, it took the form of a mass or corporate movements.[20]

But, unfortunately the instances of nonviolent resistence have not received attention and distinguished place in recorded

Pure and complete sorrow is as impossible as pure and complete joy.

Leo Tolstoy (War & Peace)

history of mankind. Historians are generally inclined towards politics and wars Albert Einstein appreciated the use of nonviolence to end the conflicts as he said "***we must learn the difficult lesson that the future of mankind will be tolerable only when our course in world affairs as well as in other matters is based on justice and law, rather than on the threat of naked power" (Einstein: on Peace and Gandhi.***[21]

Today, the world is standing at the threshold of transformation along with conflicts of religious, economic and political interests among the people of different groups and nations. Humanity is in the grip of high level terrorism all over the world. In this situation, Einstein may be remembered when he says: "We need an essentially new way of thinking if mankind is to survive. Men must radically change their attitudes towards each other and their views of the future. Force must no longer be an instrument of politics. .... Today, we do not have much time left, it is up to our generation to succeed in thinking differently. If we fail, the days of civilised humanity are numbered.[22]

Critics of 'Pacifism' believe that, perfect non-violence is impossible to practice so long as we exist physically, John Dewey criticized the early notion of Pacifism as, ***"The ordinary Pacifist's method is like trying to avoid conflict in the use of the road by telling men to love one another, instead of by instituting a rule of the road. Until Pacifism puts its faith in constructive, inventive intelligence instead of in appeal to emotions and in exhortation, the disparate unorganised forces of the world will continue to develop outbreaks of violence."***[23] Even though, Mahatma Gandhi and other pacifists provided constructive and practical approaches to the world to resolve the problems non-violently. But in the modern context of globalisation and human affairs, people are greatly apprehensive about the path of Pacifism for conflict resolution. Today human societies in the world are so structured that the policy of Pacifism creates insecurity among the believers.

In the violence ridden world, a nation or its citizens feel insecure if they are not armed properly to protect themselves. A nation disarmed could be vulnerable to attack from the armed states or nations. Thus, the approach of Pacifism, to resolve the problems of modern world, is incapable of creating confidence among the peace loving people in the violence ridden society. Though Albert Einstein a great admirer of Gandhi boosted the morale and confidence of humans when he said ***"Gandhi's non violence is a possible antidote to the massive violence unleashed by the fission of the atom."***[24]

B.R. Nanda writes in the 2001 edition of Britannica Encyclopedia that, ***"In a time, of deepening crisis in the underdeveloped world, of social malaise in the affluent societies, of the shadow of unbridled technology and the precarious peace of nuclear terror it seems likely that Gandhi's ideas and techniques will become increasingly relevant."***[25] The need of the hour is to put this relevance into action. Gandhi had evolved a holistic and very comprehensive vision of security and world peace. He had provided concrete solutions of the war, violence and conflicts in the world. Now it is high time, when people have to be taught about know how of practicing the theories of Mahatma Gandhi.

Not only Mahatma Gandhi, the teachings of great thinkers like Buddha, Mahavira, Gurunanak, Jesus Christ, Sufi saints and seers, the Gita and other holy scriptures of the world should be re-explored and revised for seeking the ways of non violent

We are now at the beginning of the planetisation of Mankind.
***Jeilhard de Chardin* (The Future of Man) New York, Harper Roxs.**

resistance as an alternative to reliance upon arms and violent methods of defence and securities. If there is violence, terrorism and war in the world, whether defensive or offensive, there will be always Pacifism to resist them by means of non-violent strategies. Pacifism will never cease in the world even if, people of the world pay it attention or not. To adopt the ways of non-violent resistance the minds of people have to be changed through training. Education may be the last strategy to inculcate the core values of life - love, compassion, oneness, forgiveness and so forth among the present generation and the next to come. This is the only option left for peaceful existence of human society.

Peace Through Education

After the First World War, thinkers felt the urgency of establishing peace in the world, hence they began to search a long term non-violent means which could establish lasting peace in the world and could protect the human society from catastrophe of wars. They felt, education must be the last approach to peace in an individual and in the world. In this connection H.G. Wells (1927) stated about the urgency of education for peace as ***"human beings are embarked upon a race between education and catastrophe.***[26] The statement implies that education must overtake the possibilities of wars. If a group of human society promote war and violence, why can't another counter part promotes peace. Promotion of peace is possible, only through education. Education in broader sense is the only strategy which can change the attitudes of people and can develop an aversion to violence and war.

Education for peace implies, drawing out from people their instincts to live peacefully with others. Education for peace emphasises ethical and moral values upon which the society should be based for its peaceful existence. Aggression is the natural instinct within human beings. Under the influence of negative forces generated by the fast track techno-scientific development of human civilisation, the instincts of aggression and destruction have been aggravated. The instincts of aggression are expressed in the form of violence and terrorism in the world. The urgent need is to control and chanellise the dangerous and injurious passions through civilised process. It is education, which can deal with both internal conflicts within human psyche and violent situations in the world. But to establish education as a successful strategy to peace, it must question the structure of violence that dominates every day life and must try to create a peaceful disposition to counteract the omnipotent values of militarism and terrorism. In this regard education has to go beyond the desposition of knowledge as Daniel Webster said, ***"Knowledge does not comprise all that is contained in the larger term of education. The feelings are to be disciplined. The passions are to be restrained, true and worthy motives are to be inspired ... And pure morality is to be inculcated in all circumstances."***[27]

If education is meant for peace it must nurture the knowledge, skills, attitudes and values that comprise a culture of peace. Education is a long term proactive strategy to promote peace in the world. The concept of Education for Peace is holistic, it embraces the physical, emotional , intellectual and social growth of person within a frame work of human values.

References

1. Krishnamurti, J. Living in Insane World. http//www.j. krishnamurti. org.Krishnamurtis teachings.

2. Preamble of the constitution of the UNESCO. www/unesco.org/ education/information.

3. Harris, Ian. M. (1988). *Peace Education* London, Mc Farland and company, Inc: Publishers, p. 8.

4. Ranganathananda (1986). *External Values for a Changing Society, Education for Human Excellence,*. Bombay, Bhartiya Vidya Bhavan,Vol. III, p. 107.

5. Blavatsky, H. (1981) *Practical Occultism* Madras, The Theosophical Publishing House, pp. 72-73.

6. Rachil, Kumar S. (2008). The Problem of Living Morally. Condensed from Theosophia, *Theosophical Digest* 20 (79). pp.13-14.

7. Ranganathanand. op. cit.

8. *Ibid.*, p. 365.

9. *Ibid.*

10. Ayandrali, Dutta (2008), A Charmed Life, Times Life of Sunday. *The Times of India,* Nov. 23.

11. *Ibid.*

12. Kumar, S. (2009). Wisdom the Great Redeemer, Condensed from *life is for living.* Chennai.Theosophical Publishing House.

13. *Ibid.*

14. *Ibid.*

15. *Ibid.*, p. 39.

16. Krishnamurti, J. Freedom from violence is true liberation, Excerpts from the book *Total Freedom* by J. Krishnamurti Times of India, 2008, Nov. 26.

17. On Bertand, Russel, http//www/en. wikipedia.org/wikei

18. Shukla, Surinder, K: Conflict Resolution and Peace Possibilities in Gandhian Perspective. http//www.gandhi foundation. net/ article/ education/htm.

19. *Ibid.*

20. Richard, B. Gregg (1938). *The Power of Non violence* Ahmedabad, Navajeevan Publishing House, preface.

21. Shukla op.cit.

22. Gangal, A. Quest for Harmony in an Age of Globalisation And Weapons of Mass Destruction http//www.the free library.com/ Mahatma Gandhi +Concepts+of+Global+Security+And+Peace

23. Dewey, John (1938). *Intelligence In the Modern World* John Dewey's Philosophies. Joseph Ratner (Ed & introduction) New York, The Modern Library, p. 495.

24. David, P. Barash and Charles P. Webel (2002). *Peace and Conflict Studies.* Thousand Oaks, Sage publications, p. 25.

25. *Ibid.*

26. Harris, op. cit., p. 16.

27. Harris, *ibid.*

4

Historical Development of Education for Peace

Madam Montessori said, ***"all education is for peace."*** Even then we find history of education entrusted with the responsibility of making secure 'peace' in the world. In 1910, an eminent American philosopher William James wrote an essay, 'The Moral Equivalent of War', "stating that educators and teachers should wage a campaign against militaristic thinking that was perverting civilization.[1]

Formally, historical development of Education for Peace began since around the First World War in 1918. The Document "Education and the People's Peace, (1943) states: ***"The World War ended with the belief that a war was fought to end the war and to make the world safe for democracy."***[2] The peoples all over the world started struggling to attain a decent and peaceful world by means, other than war because they have

The real and lasting victories are those of peace, and not of war.

Ralph Waldo Emerson-

experienced the catastrophe of war. The people began to believe that, a world is possible where men can learn to walk together in dignity and peace. After Armistice, education became the chief concern of the statesmen of the world.

In July 1919, a Peace Convention of Nations Education Association, U.S.A met in Milwaukes, United States. The convention passed strong resolutions and urged, "the creation of an International Commission on Education .... to provide for a world education in the elements of democratic citizenship and the extension of the privilege of education to all people and to all classes."[3]

Further all successive conventions favoured the establishment of the 'League of Nations' but it was intensively believed that ***"the only league of Nations that gives any assurance of a permanent peace is the league which teachers of the earth shall write in the minds and hearts of the children.***[4] All conventions faithfully reflected the optimism of the moment. The educators raised their voices and warned that, "it will be futile to .... establish a League of Nations unless there is back of peace terms and of the League of Nations, a world-citizenry. A peace founded on coercion can never survive: only a peace founded upon ... a mutuality of purpose secured through definitely planned system of education stands a chance of suriviving."[5]

The League of Nations was founded in 1920 with the hope of preserving peace in the world. But The 'League' had limited scope in resolving conflicts between nations because it was not able to successfully mediate. However the 'League of Nations Union' promoted 'Education for International Understanding' and 'Education for World Citizenship' in England. Despite, the earnest efforts of League of Nations to maintain peace in the world, the Second World War (1939-45) was fought. The whole world experienced the pain of the catastrophe of the war again. It was believed at international level that, the great war was cunningly contrived conspiracy carried to its tragic climax through an educational system. Further, it was declared that ***"Unless....... the children of all freemen are trained effectively in all of those habits and arts that make the national solidarity and strength and for international sympathy and understanding, the safety of civilization can not be guaranteed, even by the League of Nations. A world half educated will be only half free."***[6] Though emphasis was placed on the economic cause of war but it was also thought that, all mankind's hope will come crashing down again, if people fail once more to add certain educational factors to the support of peaceful organization of the world. It was believed that knowledge and attitude that are conducive to peace can be developed only by education, so are the knowledge and attitude that contain the seeds of war. It was felt that, *"by appropriate educational measures and intelligent desire for peace, with an understanding of the conditions necessary for maintaining it, must be fostered among all the people in every part of the world."*[7] But it was also believed that no nation can wisely and safely conduct such education unless all nations do so.

With aforestated conditions as a general frame work, the Document proposed the conscious and systematic use of organised education to help establish and maintain the people's peace after the peoples war. The Document emphatically declared, ***"this powerful force of education must be fully and wisely used in mankind's next and perhaps last chance to built a peaceful world."***[8] During the period of World War II people of world community, with growing clarity of vision, started thinking in the direction of achieving a growing measure of freedom and fair play of all men. The whole purpose of struggle changed from a defensive to a creative basis. They strived to seek long-term measures to stop the war and terminate the fear of catastrophe and violence in the world. Consequently amidst ideological commotions, United Nations Organisation (UNO) was founded in January, 1942. It was a coalition to resist the aggression of the axis of powers in World War II formed of 26 nations initially. In 1945, original membership was formed of 51 states. Today, there are 192 member states.

The Charter of UN enumerated measures for the prevention of war and removal of threats to peace in the World. The founding of the United Nations provided an impetus for an international effort to teach about the problems associated with war, violence, injustice, illiteracy, poverty and other sources of human conflicts. In keeping with the principles of the UN Charter, that promoted international co-operation and peace, the United Nations Educational Scientific and Cultural Organisation (UNESCO) was founded in November 1945 as a specialised UN agency and set in motion with the objectives: to contribute to peace and security by promoting collaboration among the nations through education, science and culture in order to further universal respect for justice, for the rule of the law and for the human rights and fundamental freedom which are affirmed for the peoples of the world without distinction of race, sex, language or religion by the Charter of the United Nations (UNESCO, 2004).[9]

The UNESCO was assigned the tasks of advancing through the educational, scientific and cultural relations of the people of the world, the objectives of international peace and of the common welfare of mankind for which United Nations Organization was established and which its Charter proclaimed. Hence the preamble of the constitution of the UNESCO reflected

I do not want the peace that passeth understanding. I want the understating which bringeth peace.

Helen Keller-

it's motto as: ***Since war begins in the minds of man, it is in the minds of men that the defence of peace must be constructed.***[10]

Since it's inception, UNESCO is carrying out its mission according to the terms of its Constitution which was created to build a world from which the specter of war has to be banished. The last six decades have witnessed several significant advocacies by UNESCO for Education for Peace. UNESCO has taken problem focused actions to reinforce peace from three stand points, which are mutually complementary: peace research, study of the international system and lastly education for peace, which concerns both the development of international understanding by means of education and the most diversified forms of action to promote an awareness among all sectors of society, such as to encourage the radical changes of attitude and practice which the institution of a peaceful world calls for.[11]

To promote peace and international understanding, UNESCO launched ASPnet in 1953, which in 2003 included 7500 institutions ranging from nursery schools to teacher training institutions in 170 countries. The network is dedicated to the pursuit of peace, liberty justice and human development. The other major actions of UNESCO which are two of the landmarks are recommendations on education for international understanding, peace, human rights and fundamental freedom (1974) and action plan (1994) for education for peace, human rights and democracy endorsed by 144 countries.

An innovative pilot project on "Peace and Disarmament Education" is being implemented in four countries Albania, Niger, Peru and Cambodia. By UN Department of Disarmament Affairs (UNDDA) and Hague Appeal for Peace (HAP). The Centre for Research on Education for Peace (CERPE) at the University of Haifa, Israel, which has been functionary since 1998 serves as an interdisciplinary and international forum for the scholarly studies of education for peace. The centre has undertaken a number of research projects on Education for Peace. The Earth and Peace Education Associates International (EPE) New York, is yet another organisation which promotes basic values related to peace, viz., sustainability, non-violence, social justice, intergeneration equity and participatory decision-making. Besides these, a number of other organizations, national and international, governmental and non-governmental around the world are working for peace.

Much of the peace research that has been carried out in recent years is the work of NGOs established either as national or international centres. Many of them are federated in the International Peace·Research Association (IPRA), which has consultative status with UNESCO and was affiliated to the International Social Science Council, in 1999, United Nations General Assembly approved that, we are at present half way through the decade for the promotion of culture of peace. On the eve of the new millennium (21st Century) the General Assembly of the United Nations proclaimed the year 2000 as International Year for the Culture of Peace and the decade 2001-2010 as the International Decade for Culture of Peace and Non-Violence for the Children of the World.

The notion of a "Culture of Peace" was first elaborated for UNESCO at the 'International Congress on Peace in the Minds of Men' held at Yamoussoukro, cote d Ivories in 1989. The Yamoussoukro Declaration called on UNESCO to ***"construct a new vision of peace by developing a peace culture based on the universal values of respect for life, liberty, justice,***

Nations who relieved on their defensive forces and armament factories for peace keeping should shift focus on long terms, preventive action-building peace through education.

Federico Mayer (UNESCO Director General)-

solidarity, tolerance, human rights and equality between women and men and to promote education and research for this vision.[12]

Subsequently, UNESCO World Conference on Higher Education was organised in Paris, October 1998, to build a landmark in the development of education for peace. The suit was followed by 'A Conference on Higher Education for Peace' held in Tromso, Norway, May 2000.[13] The Tromso Conference focused on certain issues, as supremacy of races and war and further endeavored to seek solutions to issues of how the peace aspect might be focused on in higher education. The Conference tried to settle down the questions regarding concept of peace education, the content and methods of peace education focusing in particular on higher education and its impact on the whole field of education, formal and informal from universities to day-care centres and communities. The Conference suggested for such methods of education, which enable and motivate the students to take part in practical peace efforts.[14]

According to the Declaration and Programme of Action for a Culture of Peace, adopted by United Nations General Assembly (1999), NGOs and other civil society organisations were urged to contribute to a global movement for a culture of peace. In response, at the midpoint of the decade, i.e. 2005, 700 civil society organisations reported to the General Assembly that the global movement is advancing despite lack of attention from the mass media.

Since 2001 various national NGOs coalitions in several countries have been established to promote the culture of peace and non-violence.

Education for Peace in India

History of Indian Education reveals that education in India has been always for peace. In ancient India, when teachers in gurukulas used to invoke for blessings before their discourses, this invocation was a Peace Chant (Santipatha). The Peace Invocation was found common in Upanishadic education. It is as follows:

> ***Om, Sahanavavatu, Sahanau bhunaktu***
> ***Sahaviryam karvavahai;***
> ***Tejasvinavadhita mastu;***
> ***ma vidivisavahai,***
> ***Om, Santih, Santih, Santih-***

Om! may God protect us (teacher and students) both! May God nourish us both! May we both acquire energy (as a result of this study)! May we both become illumined (by this study)! May we not hate each other! Om Peace! Peace! Peace!

"The peace invocation contains many beautiful sentiments, the sentiments which have inspired Indian education – secular and religious for a few thousand years. Teachers and students engaged in the pursuit of knowledge and excellence of character in education. It is a co-operative endeavour between the student and the teacher. The invocation expresses the idea of education as the achievement of knowledge and excellence of character in the context of a harmonious relationship between the teacher and student. The giving and receiving of knowledge leading to the remaking of man depends on the stimulus of such teacher-student relationship. The teacher gives and student receives, not only ideas and informations but inspiration as well."[15] Hence, the education in Upanishadic style begin with a prayer for peace within and without. This invocation is called Santipath or Peace Chant, because it is meant to induce a state of creative tranquility in the mind by making it receptive, knowledge oriented and bereft of hatred and other evil passions.

In ancient India, the theme of education was the real nature of man and his true destiny; and education was meant to investigate the inner world of experience. Through education man reached the stage of maturity of outlook and he was prepared to discipline his emotions and to deal with the pressures of the external world.

The ancient Indian education primarily struck the idea of keeping a human body, an excellence venue for spiritual enlightenment, thus it prescribed the techniques of Yoga as an integral part of education. Julian Huxley called it **the science of human possibilities.**[16] It was believed that the practice of Yoga harmonises body, mind and soul. It transforms the personality of a man and provides him farsight and foresight to life and strength and steadiness to character. When a man realises his real nature, all fears of set-backs are completely removed and burnt in the fire of spiritual knowledge and he attains a stable moral life. Apart from aforesaid expositions, there are thousands of examples in Indian history which reveal how ancient education was intertwined with peace values.

Not only spiritual life, but also religion was the centre of all educational discourses. It was the mundane concern of education which emphasised on the relationship between man and man, man and the nature, man and the society, man and the universe.

'Sarve Bhavantu Sukhinah' and 'Vasudhaiva Kutubakam' have been the basic themes of our educational system. But with the passage of time, as history descended, the values inherent in Indian education began to decline towards the mundane surface and slowly occupied more and more materialistic ground. British period of education created a big gap between ancient and modern; the values interwined in educational system were deliberately made to fade out. The British period marked a hiatus in the history of Indian education. In 1884, the government dismissed the inclusion of moral education in the curriculum. The attitude of the British Raj was negative even antagonistic to religious and moral education.

After a long interval of time, the Report of the Central Advisory Board (1944-46) however marked a departure in the thinking on the subject. It recognised that "religion in the widest sense inspires all education and that a curriculum devoid of ethical basis will prove barren in the end. Further a special Committee under the chairmanship of Bishop G.D. Barne was appointed to study the feasibility of implementing the recommendation of the Central Advisory Board. The Committee came to the conclusion that religious education should be "the responsibility of the home and community to which pupils belong.[17]

After independence, the Report of Secondary Education Commission (1952-53) was a significant landmark in the direction of moral and religious education. The Commission identified character building as the defining goal of education. The Report prescribed 'moral instruction' as the means to achieve this goal. It recommended integrative approach to moral instruction rather than treating it as a separate subject. The Report stipulated that, religious instructions may be given in schools only on a voluntary basis and outside the regular school hours, such instruction being confined to the children of the particular faith concerned and given with the consent of the parents and the managements.[18] Reviews of the Report reveal that, it had lack of confidence in implementing its recommendation on moral religious instruction. Later on, the Report of The University Education. Commission, (1962) put forward the issue more confidently: "If we exclude spiritual training in our institutions...we would be untrue to our whole historical

Establishing lasting peace is the work of education; all politics can do is keep us out of war.

Maria Mantessri-

development. The Report recommended not for moral or religious education, rather it marked for evolving "a national faith, a national way of life based on the Indian outlook on religion, free from dogmas, rituals and assertions"[19]

The Education Commission (1964-66) emphasised on education and national development and pointed out the defects of the curriculum as the "absence of provision for education in social, moral and spiritual values."[20] It recommended that, 'these value should be taught with help, wherever possible, of the ethical teachings of great religions.

The National Policy on Education (1986) expressed concern over the erosion of essential values and increasing cynicism in the society and it recommended for making education, ***"a forceful tool for the cultivation of social and moral values .... Education should foster universal and eternal values, oriented towards the unity and integration of our people"[21].***

The Programme of Action (1992) attempted to integrate the different components of value education into the curriculum of education at all stages of school education.

The National Curriculum Framework for School Education (NCERT, 1975-2000) adopted value-oriented approach to integrate peace concern in education specially, the National Curriculum Frame Work (2000) pleaded for integrating value education into the curriculum, and stated that, what is required however "is not religious education but education about religions, their basics, the values inherent in them and also a comparative study of the philosophy of all religions."[22] The framework prescribed that value education and education about religions should be Judiciously integrated with all subjects of study.[23]

In India, struggle for value oriented education through a decade has shifted its focus from moral and religious education to 'Education for Peace' in larger context. Recently The National Curriculum Framework (2005) made a major change in approach and considered the 'Education for Peace, the ideal strategy for contextualsing and operationalising values in education.

NCERT took the reference of The UNESCO World Conference on Higher Education, Paris, (1998) when a country paper entitled, 'Higher Education in India, Vision and Action' was presented by Indian National Commission for Co-operation with UNESCO, New Delhi, and envisaged the status of teacher as it is increasingly recognised that if defence of peace are to be built in the minds of men and women and if qualities of co-operation, mutuality and harmony are to be fostered in humanity, the role of teachers will include the task of changing the tendencies of egoism, domination and war. It is particularly for this reason that a new programme of teachers training has to be envisaged and this programme will not only cater to the continuous development of professional skills but also continuous development of teachers ethical and spiritual abilities.

Keeping in view, the context of The UNESCO World Conference (1998) and Education for Peace, the Curriculum Framework (2005) recognised the role of teachers as very important and found its specific relevance as they are the role models for students and they not only impart knowledge but can also influence the psychological, emotional and spiritual growth of their students. A teacher is the only person who can create an environment for the induction and transaction of peace to the their students through education. Hence, NCERT has organised various orientation and training programmes for teacher educators, on various issues and concerns related to the education for peace. NCERT is aiming to help teacher educators understand their roles as peace educators and enable them to learn the ways of integrating peace in teaching learning activities in and out of classrooms in teachers training institutions. It is hoped that the future teacher prepared under the training of such teacher educators will be able to deliver education for peace in the reality of classrooms in the schools.

Other than governmental efforts, many non-governmental institutions are working for the promotion of peace. Some of the prominent institutions are, The Gandhi Peace Foundation, The Gandhi Smriti Darshan Samiti, Gandhian Institute of Studies, Jaipur Peace Foundation, Krishnamurti Fundation, Brahma Kumai's World Spiritual University and Adhyatmika Ishwariya Vishwavidyalaya (Mount Abu, Rajasthan), Raj Yoga Education and Research Foundation, Brahmakumaris Academy, Women Shanti Sena (a peace organization) New Delhi, International Network of Museum for Peace, Gandhi Memorial Museum, Indian Institute for Peace, National Gandhi Museum, National Museum of Indian Freedom Movement, Global Peace Works, New Delhi. The UNESCO Chair in Peace, Human Rights and Democracy at Maharashtra Academy of Engineering and Education and so many other peace organizations, national and international are voluntarily working for the promotion of the culture of peace. Although NGOs have been contributing to different aspects of peace studies viz, human rights, gender discrimination, environment, individual and societal peace and so forth, they do not impart education adequately at various stages due to lack of coordination. Hence, there is need for coordination among NGOs and the educational system in India, in order to enhance the effectiveness of their proposed measures for the cause of peace and for the development of education for peace.[24]

References

1. Harris, Ian M (1988) *Peace Education,* London, Mc. Farland & Company, Inc. Publisher. p. 1.

2. EPC, NEA and AASA (1943) Education and the Peoples Peace A Report of Educational Policies Commission, National Education Association of United States and American Association of School Administration, Washington D.C. p. 1.

3. *Ibid.*, p.7.

4. *Ibid.*, p. 7.

5. *Ibid.*, p. 8.

6. *Ibid.*, p. 8.

7. *Ibid.*, p. 11.

8. *Ibid.*, p. 14.

9. UNESCO (2004), From Worldmark Encyclopedia of Nations (2007) http//www. Encyclopedia.com/doc.

10. UNESCO, Preamble (1945), http//www/unesco.org/education/ information.

11. UNESCO Report:(1977), *Thinking ahead, Unesco and the Challenges of today and tomorrow* Paris, Unesco, p. 67.

12. UNESCO and A Culture of peace, Unesco publishing www. unesco. org/cpp/uk/news.html.

13. Higher Education for Peace (2000), A conference on Higher Education for Peace, Tromso, Norway May, 2000 http//www/ peace 2vit,no/netp/cotribution/ ole-mjos/papers/ole-mjos

14. Mjos, O.D (2000), University shall speak Peace unto all the world. http//www.times higher education.co.UK/

15. Ranganathananda (1985) *THE MESSAGE OF THE UPANISADS, An Exposition of The Upanisads In the Light of*

Modern Thought And Modern Needs, Bombay, Bhartiya Vedya Bhavan.

16. Ranganathananad (1986). *Eternal Values for A Changing Society*, Bombay, Bhartiya Vidya Bhavan, p. 142.

17. NCERT (2006) National Curriculum Frame Work (2005), *EDUCATION FOR PEACE, Position Paper, National Focus Group on Education For Peace*, New Delhi NCERT, pp. 6-7.

18. *Ibid*, p. 7.

19. *Ibid.*

20. *Ibid.*

21. *Ibid.*

22. *Ibid.*

23. *Ibid.*

24. *Ibid.*, p. 6.

5

Education for Peace: What does it Really Mean?

The word 'education' is derived from the Latin word 'educare' which means to draw out from within. Thus "education for peace" implies drawing out from people their instincts to live peacefully with others and emphasises peace values upon which a society should be based.[1]

In India, the word, 'Shiksha' is derived from Sanskrit word 'Shiksh' which means teaching-learning or giving-receiving. In this sense, education for peace is the communication or transaction of human values which are essential for peaceful state of the individual and the society. The process of transaction or communication of human values occurs in between the teacher and the taught.

In ancient India, Shiksha was not merely a transaction of information rather it was 'Vidya' or wisdom which the teacher used to transmit to his students for the pursuit of knowledge

Education is the fundamental method of social progress and reform.

John Dewey-

and excellence of character. Through Vidya (para and apara) students reached the stage of maturity (or a stage where a man has sufficient wisdom to decide, what is wrong and what is right.) and they were trained enough not only to develop their inner spiritual self but to contribute to the welfare of the society.

As history shows, education in ancient India was interwoven with values such as Let all be happy (Sarve Bhavantu Sukhinah), whole world is a family (Vasudhaiva Kutumbakam), non-violence (Ahimsa)) and code of righteous conduct (Dharma) to promote and maintain peace in the society. This education in real sense was the education for peace.

Before elaborating the concept of education for peace, it is essential to know the conceptual difference between Peace Education and Education for Peace.

As far as Peace Education is concerned, it is a specific subject different from other subjects of studies and deals with the issues as:

- the internal conflict within the human psyche and violent situations in the outer world
- cause of war
- prevention of war
- international understanding
- creative solutions of conflicts
- human rights
- violent nature of the societies

Education for Peace assumes peace in Education.

Maynus Haavelsrud-

- structural violence in the society
- history of peace efforts
- present status of peace movements
- proposed future efforts to achieve peace

An American peace educator, Betty Reardon defines Peace Education as : ***"Peace education is a learning intended to prepare the learner to contribute towards the achievement of peace."***[2] This definition implies that, 'Peace Education' teaches skills of peace making. It teaches the affective domain of personality and enables a person to resolve his tensions and problems of everyday life. Peace Education has been practiced informally throughout the world in different forms from hundreds of years. It was originated in the western world as, 'Pacifism in Christianity and practice of non-violence by the 'Quakers' in England. In the east, teachings of Buddha, Mahavira, Gurunanak, Sufi saints and seers, Bhagwad Gita and other Indian Scriptures are examples of Peace Education. Mahatma Gandhi, who is recognised as a Pacifist in the eastern world, and his followers discovered the dynamic ways to apply non-violence (ahimsa) in the political struggle, Satyagraha and Non-Cooperation movement are such examples. He also emphasised on the non-violent means to solve everyday problems of individuals as well.

In the last two and half decades, people have used educational means to promote the causes of peace-movements, which later on took the form of 'Peace Education'. The people who were interested and associated with peace actions and wanted to find the solutions for the violent behaviours in the society and to bring peace in the world, turned their interests to 'Peace Education'. Now, in the context of modern world where human society is in the grip of ever increasing violence and terrorism, Peace Education as a separate subject or discipline is not effective enough to achieve the purpose of promoting peace in the world.

Despite past efforts of Peace Education to promote peace in the society and to eliminate the probability of war and violence from the world, no war and violence have been eliminated rather their frequency and probability are increasing everyday. Thus, it is thought today that 'Peace Education' as a separate subject is not a very effective strategy in promoting the culture of peace among people. A separate subject is a matter of choice; people have option to choose or not to choose. Most of the people do not have interest in, and awareness of the subject. A large section of students at higher education level is ignorant about the subject. Peace Education in general, has not been included in the curriculum of higher education, though it could have been infused in the subjects of Humanities, Social Sciences and the Natural Sciences. Hence, the failure of past efforts to promote peace through education have created anxiety among the governments, policy makers and educationists all over the world. However, it can not be denied that, due to various efforts in the past and in the present, people have somehow acquired awareness and understanding of various issues related to peace as, war and catastrophe, cause of wars, violation of human rights, international understanding, structural violence and exploitations in the society, equality of opportunities and so forth. Awareness of these issues have caused various struggles for justice and demands for human rights. Intermingling of knowledge and various influences of global change and material development have created a new type of fermentation and unrest,

A lot of students don't want to take it. They said that they did'nt want to think about a nuclear holocaust, that they had to get on with their career.

Henry T. Nash- (Thinking About the unthinkable)-

rather chaotic situations in the communities. Hence, man in the present world is in a state of dilemma.

High pace material development has destroyed the physical and human environment and moreover, has dehumanised men. Today, mankind is experiencing a great threat to their survival due to ever expected nuclear war, horrible shows of global terrorism and heinous violence. Thus, the present perspective of human existence calls for a strategy that is more effective than 'Peace Education' in removing the fear of war and terrorism from the world and protect the people from various types of exploitations in the human society. There is a great need of a strategy which could change the attitude of people and equip them with knowledge and skills of 'Peace Making' in their local communities, in the nation and in the world in the larger context. In the present context of a turbulent world where probabilities of war, terrorism and various types of violence are increasing day by day, where human survival and sustenance of human society is at stake, Education for Peace is considered the last approach and long term strategy to secure peace in this world.

Education for Peace: Concept and Meaning

Education for peace contextualises the teaching learning process. In simple language, 'Education for Peace' provides a context or environment where enterprise of education or teaching - learning should take place.

Today, the perspective of teaching learning has been totally changed, perhaps it is badly affected by high pace development and modern pragmatic approach to life. In the present period of globalisation, marketisation and invasion of a permissive philosophy, men's unchecked actions and

School is both a child and mother of warfare ideology.

Jaime Diaz-

uncontrolled desires have spoiled the human environment and dehumanised men. Educational institutions are very much affected by the negative forces emerging from malicious environment all around. It is serious and unavoidable concern that schools, colleges and university campuses which are meant to nurture the ideals of peace, have been housing violence. Everyday, we are freshened with the news of kidnapping, murder, rape, suicide and other types of violence in educational institutions. Today children use violent language, play violent games, sing and dance violently, vulgarity has become a fashion today. It is general belief that, the sources of violence are the homes and the society from where children are coming. Today children are vulnerable to violence. If they don't get conducive environment for their emotional development, they will turn into terrorists, murderers or any type of anti-social persons. In this perspective, home has to play a major role in protecting their children from violent impulses by providing them emotional support, communicative environment and a sense of togetherness and belongingness in their homes. Since, education has a large share in the development of children hence it cannot deny its responsibility to prepare a child or individual to meet the challenges and pressures of the modern world.

Education for peace provides a perspective for organising and planning the whole system of education. As contrary to peace education, it implies blending or interweaving of human values with the whole process of education. In other terms, Education for Peace contextualises the teaching learning process. It integrates peace concerns in education.

Education for Peace is supposed to be the ideal strategy for contextualising and operationalising ethical and moral values

The purposes of schooling is to broden and enrich the minds and hearts of students so that they can shape their own values and arrives at their own judgment.

Michall Siler (Value Education)

in the educational process. In this framework of education, peace becomes the shaping vision of education. This implies a paradigm shift in the total transaction of education. Today the enterprise of education is totally driven by the market forces. Education for Peace is not against the market but it does not recognise the market as the sole aim of education. The market is a part of our worldly life but not life as a whole. Education for Peace is the education for a complete life; it's endeavor is holistic; it is not merely a training for earning bread and butter rather; it equips individuals with values, attitudes and skills, to become a wholesome persons.[3] Thus Education for Peace trains a person to live in harmony with others. It's goal is to develop individuals into responsible citizens. Now in the present perspective, education for peace is entrusted with the task of promoting a culture of peace. This is the new vision of peace, which was originated in the International Congress on Peace in the Minds of Men, held at Yamoussoukro, Cote d' Ivoire in 1989. The Congress for the first time elaborated the notion of a Culture of Peace for the UNESCO. The Yamoussoukro Declaration called on UNESCO to construct a new vision of peace by developing a peace culture based on the universal values, respect for life, liberty, justice, solidarity, tolerance, human rights and equality between women and men and to promote education and research for this vision.[4]

Subsequently in 1997 the United Nations General Assembly proclaimed the first decade of the 21st century and the third millennium, the years 2001 to 2010 as the 'International Decade for the Promotion of a Culture of Peace and Non-Violence for the Children of the World.[5]

The Hague Agenda for Peace and Justice for the 21st century was the first significant step to promote Education for Peace. The foremost principles of the Agenda were the necessity of instituting systematic education for peace, to support the

United Nations Decade for a Culture of Peace and Non-Violence for the Children of the World and to introduce peace and human rights education into all educational institutions, including medical and law schools.[6]

The U.N. Declaration had made the landmark around which people could mobilise for fundamental change. The Declaration acclaimed that: "Access to education and various forms of learning is necessary but not sufficient condition for a 'Culture of Peace'. A Comprehensive system of education and training is needed for all groups of people at all levels and forms of education, both formal and non-formal. The development of a holistic approach, based on participatory methods and taking into account the various dimensions of education for a culture of Peace (i.e. peace and non-violence, human rights, democracy, tolerance, international and intercultural understanding, cultural and linguistic diversity) as its main objectives. [7]

To achieve the objective, it was expected that Department of Education for Culture of Peace will, in cooperation with other programme sectors of UNESCO

- monitor the implementation of standard-setting instruments and plans of action;
- Implement national plans and programmes relating to education for a culture of peace;
- encourage improvement and innovations related to curricula, contents and teaching methods, pedagogical materials and also the training of teachers and other educational staff;
- encourage bilateral and multilateral cooperation to revise history and geography text books;
- promote the linguistic diversity at all educational levels;

- strengthen the UNESCO Associated School Project Network (ASPnet);
- promote physical education and sports for a culture of peace.

In the context of the Declaration of U.N. General Assembly, promoting 'Culture of Peace' involves two pronged strategy: one that the members of a society need to be oriented towards peace instead of violence, the other that the social, economic and political systems have to be reoriented to peace at the same time. Besides UNESCO, other important and active advocate of Education for Peace is UNICEF.

UNICEF describes Education for Peace as that education which

- Functions as 'Zone of peace' where children are safe from violent conflicts;
- Upholds children's basic rights as outlined by CRC (Convention on the Rights of Child);
- Develops a climate that models peaceful and respectful behaviour among all members of the learning community;
- Demonstrates the principles of equality and non-discrimination in administrative policies and practices;
- Draws on the knowledge of peace-building that exists in the community, including means of dealing with conflict that are effective, non-violent and rooted in the local culture;
- Handle conflicts in ways that respect the rights and dignity of all involved.[8]

Hence in this respect, Education for Peace provides a new perspective to educational process which implies that, teaching-learning should be carried out from peace perspective. The peace perspective involves certain conditions as, children are safe from violent conflicts; their rights are preserved; learning climate is peaceful where principles of equality and non-discrimination are followed by administrative staff and policy makers; knowledge of non-violent methods of conflict resolutions and peace building rooted in local culture is provided to learning community; and finally teaching learning takes place in an environment of mutual respect for rights and dignity of all people involved.

Thus Education for Peace assumes 'peace' as a context. It is an appropriate and pedagogically gainful point of coherence for human values. Without such frame work, integration of values into educational process is impossible. Hence Education for Peace is supposed to be an ideal strategy for contextualising and operationalising value education. It provides experiences to children and youth through which they internalise values. But this process of experiential learning is not possible in the present frame-work of education where teaching is classroom centred and purely cognitive in nature.[9] Education for Peace calls for the liberty of teaching-learning process from the confines of class rooms. It is expected that the education organised in such a way is hopefully going to remove the deficiencies of learning community regarding emotional, social and relational skills to meet the challenges of the modern world.

Approach to Education for Peace

The approach to Education for Peace is different from that of Peace Education or separate subject approach from psychological, pedagogical and motivational points of view. If we want to educate children or individuals for peace, the emphasis cannot be merely on acquisition of knowledge rather on the teaching-learning process through which, a 'culture of peace' may be promoted. Since 'peace' is an all embracing concept, it is to be integrated in all the activities, curricular and co-curricular in the schools To blend all educational processes with peace and to maximise its effects, the teacher-taught interactions, lessons in text books and the total environment in the schools or educational institutions have to be peace oriented. But how is it possible? Further questions arise-how can a culture of peace be created to shape the enterprise of education how can a culture of peace be translated in to practice? In response to these obvious questions, inherent nature of Education for Peace should be well understood. Thus Education for Peace implies a commitment not only to a certain educational content or curriculum but to a pedagogy that gives teachers and students an opportunity to practice some of the values that Education for Peace is concerned about transmitting.

Education for Peace relies on the strategy which is more than class-room teaching-learning, about certain concepts and events related to Peace presented in text books, rather it is concretisation of peace in to action. It means that education for peace can not and should not be delivered in the conventional mode of teaching-learning. Its success solely relies on it is pedagogy. Despite all necessary conditions to deliver Education for Peace, the foremost and important pre-condition is the 'will' or desire for peace among the people concerned. No culture of peace could be created without the Will for Peace. Thus the first step in this direction would be to induce the Will among the people concerned with education that is, the members of the society, governments, politicians, policy makers and all people involved in the total process of education from higher education to nursery and ultimately to day care schools. In the past history, education failed several times in promoting 'peace' because it was not attempted full heartedly and with a strong will. Hence 'will' should be translated into concrete actions and all the members of society should join hands and hearts to promote the culture of peace.

The next step would be; designing of the curriculum, writing of text books and lastly the transaction of values blended in curricular and co-curricular activities in and out of the class room.

Curriculum Design

The pedagogic strategy for Education for Peace presupposes the integration of values and ideals in all educational activities in and out of the classrooms. In the broader sense, integration occurs when all the activities of the schools and colleges, curricular and co-curricular are geared towards Education for Peace. At the classroom level, peace dimensions are woven into the contents of the lessons. The lessons are designed in such a way that could help students to imbibe peace values.

The integration of peace concepts or peace dimensions in the existing course content is also called infusion of peace concepts and peace values in already prescribed curricula. Infusion is the preferred method for teachers to get started with Education for Peace at the elementary and secondary level, and even at the college and university level, where teachers already have prescribed curriculum and there is very little or no room for extra course.

Infusion does not require teachers to develop new courses and hence may not be time consuming. Infusion also does not require getting permission from the school principal or administrator and head of the departments at the university level. Teachers have relative autonomy in their classrooms to decide what and how they want to teach.[10] To infuse peace concepts, present curricula may be altered by introducing new topics or develop new approaches or even to initiate new programmes.

At the college and university level, more advanced and special courses dealing with war, terrorism, nuclear issues, environmental destruction and non-violence may be appropriately designed. However, infusion of peace concerns in various courses which are already existing in the universities, can work quite well. Faculty from many different fields or disciplines can find ways to investigate the problems of violence and determinants of peace in their respective courses. Every discipline can provide examples related to peace and conflict topics. Every teacher can infuse peace and justice concepts by using his or her own imagination to tailor the content to a particular group of students.[11] Almost in all subjects, teacher can find space to infuse peace concepts. Infusing peace and justice concepts into traditional school activities or in to the conventional activities of universities allow students to think about the causes of important wars and pervading terrorism, their catastrophic effects and peace dilemmas which are perverting our civilisation.

Today, another approach to curriculum design have been borrowed from constructivist psychology. Presently constructivist psychology has influenced the teaching – learning process. It has established that children construct knowledge holistically. If knowledge is presented in appropriate contexts, it becomes more meaningful and enjoyable for children. In the integrated approach, lessons and topics become the means to convey peace messages in meaningful contexts. This approach motivates students to learn and to relate the learnt subject matters to their own life. They get contexts and connections to explore, think, reflect, and internalise positive tendencies. Hence it implies that, total curriculum framework must reflect the integration of peace values. In totality every teacher should become 'peace educator'. In schools or to say in educational institutions, classroom interactions between teacher and

If we are to teach real Peace in the world we shall have to begin with children.

Mahatma Gandhi-

students, text books, lessons, teaching methodology, school or college management, heads of the institutions, teaching and non-teaching staffs, all must be oriented to peace building.

Stage-Specific Approach to Curriculum Development

Education for peace is the education for complete life. It is not limited to the confines of classrooms, rather children's experience outside class-rooms play major role in shaping their personality as peaceful individuals. The outside experiences limit the role of teachers and peace educators. The Education for Peace, to be effective, begins in home where parents play a key role in raising peace loving children.

If children experience the possibility of peace through non-violent conflict resolutions at the family level, their faith in the possibility for peace and willingness to work for it at different levels grows.[12] Children need assurance from their parents that the world will be all right, change is possible and that they can help bring about change. Parents can teach their children methods of survival and strategies for change in a society filled with violence, injustice and exploitations. Parents should not exaggerate informations provided by media and news channels regarding terrorism, war and violence, rather they can provide accurate information to their children about news events dealing with such matters. Parents should not force discussions of violent events upon young children but should rather listen carefully to children's fears and respond in a sensitive manner to their children's anxieties about violence in the world.[13] Parents who want to raise peaceful children can provide peaceful models by never using personal violence, e.g. spanking but rather by taking

Young children need help in understanding the complexity of the world order so that they may have bases for reacting intelligently to its problems as they grow older.

Judith V. Tourney **(Political Socialization Research in United States)-**

time to explain the natural consequence of certain actions. Spanking teachers provoke children to use physical violence to resolve disagreements. Since conflict is an inevitable part of life, hence children need to learn in their families to take the feelings of other people into account to deal constructively with conflict.

Parents should create a system of cooperation in the family because it is said, "Violence is nurtured by excessive competition. Non-violence on the other hand, springs from cooperation."[14] Children who grow up to become an agent of non-violent social change come from homes where there is an emotional closeness. A conducive home environment for the development of peaceful child consists of greater harmony, motivation, efficiency, children and parents sharing life together, happiness, communication, discovery of one's worth and potential. Warm home relationships with intellectual stimulation and information about current events, provide experiences that enable children to face the world confidently.[15]

Education for peace in formal sense can meet the needs of all children and youth from day care centres or early childhood stage to the stage of higher education. To serve the purpose, stage specific approach to curriculum design should be used.

Early Childhood stage

Piaget's theory of cognitive development of children may help teachers to decide when and how to present war, violence and peace concepts to children. Erikson's theory of personal and social development should also be followed in designing curriculum at early childhood. At his stage, children have peculiar

The primary task of education for peace is therefore, to reveal and top all those energies and impulses that make possible the full human capacity for meaningful and life enhancing existence.

I an M. Harris-

types of fears, such as fears of being lost, bitten or injured. They are exposed to frightening images on television, in books or in their own day to day lives. Their wild imaginations make them worried about being attacked by ferocious animals, being in dark, losing their parents, being abandoned or going upto high places.[16]

Thus, at early childhood stage parents and teachers should remove the fear of children by modeling negative reactions to frightening situations. Since children have tendency to imitate the actions of another persons like parents or teachers and they acquire their characteristics. The children recognise their parents and teachers, their role model and adopt the model's opinions and mannerisms. Hence at his stage, the examples of peaceful behaviour established by teachers, parents and other significant role models can play an important role in helping them to develop as peaceful persons.

Teachers and parents may choose songs, fables, films etc., to expose children to pleasing and peaceful experiences, to counterbalance the experiences of competition, aggression or violence which children get from other sources as television, movies, peers, school, etc.

In child care centres and kindergartens, children are not expected to see the world from another person's point of view, therefore subjects like social studies should be avoided at this stage, young children should be given opportunities to make

Our entire educational apparatus was avowedly brought into being precisely for the purpose of providing youth with indispensable knowledge about the world in which they must live. They, as we, have right to know the facts. If schools fail to implement this right, they fail to fulfill the central purpose for which they come into being.

Willard Jacobsen, Betty Reardon and Douglas Sloon-

their own choices. Since they are not able to think about implications of their choice, hence teacher should help children learn to predict the consequences of their actions.

Children of age four to six years may generally be scared of the events they see or what they hear on the news or read in comic books or watch on cartoons, while not understanding if fully. These young children need to be reassured by their parents and teachers that they are safe in the world and elders take care of their future and they will make the world safe and all right for children.

Children at this stage need to accept diversity by learning about different cultures and understanding their own backgrounds. They should be taught about, why people are different. An awareness and appreciation of the diversity of individual and collective values may lead them to non-violent resolution of conflict. This is the stage when children are required to learn caring and sharing, to understand the interdependence of people, to value cooperation and to develop a sense of community.[17]

Elementary Stage

Children at the elementary stage enter the concrete operational level of thinking; they start making moral judgments that take into account the interests of others. Children start considering more than one aspect of a situation while drawing conclusions; it means they are now ready for logical thinking. Thus elementary stage in the life of a child is the right time for laying the foundation of peace oriented personality. This is the

The scope of current higher education in India and the world outside is severely restricted , due to its undue stress on learning to do' it has to be widened to include also learning to be.

Swami Ranganathananda-

formative period of personality. As our ancient Indian education has emphasised, the early years of children's life are meant to grasp the 'sanskars'. This is the right stage when ***"teachers on the earth can write the message of peace in the hearts and minds of children".***[18] A thinker has said, ***"if you don't teach peace to a child, other can teach him violence."***

At the elementary stage, the values that form the personality are; hygiene (both of self and surrounding), obedience to elders, respect for others and elders, dignity of labour, love, compassion, honesty, tolerance, punctuality, regularity and responsibility etc. Later childhood stage would be an ideal time to include the subjects as international institutions (United Nations, UNESCO etc), world order, cultural differences, civil rights, human rights and various environmental issues befitting this age of child in the curriculum.

Children should not be burdened by the load of text books and home work, rather they should be helped to enjoy and celebrate the diversity, beauty and harmony in the nature. Children should be helped to develop their aesthetic sensibility, art of listening and sense of responsibility.

Inspite of text contents, more and more discussion about individual attitudes and beliefs that present different points of view should be encouraged to promote critical thinking among children. In the middle childhood years, children may benefit from values clarification exercises that help analyse the values that underlie beliefs and actions. Value clarification exercises can help children express their changing attitudes and establish their beliefs about peace and justice issues.[19]

If there must be trouble let it be in my day, that my child may have peace.

Thomas Paine-

Secondary Stage

Children at this stage become ready to grasp abstract thinking. Hence they should be helped to think rationally and relationally about 'What is happening in their surroundings. Teachers and adults working with children at this age have to think about how to make them aware of the problems the world faces. Young children need help to understand the complexity of the world order so that they may have a basis for reacting intelligently to its problems as they grow older.[20]

Thus at the secondary stage, children need to be equipped with the competency and understanding of values underlying democracy, equality justice, human rights, human dignity and so forth so that they could respond positively to cultural diversity and peaceful co-existence in the society. This is the right stage for the development of skills, creative thinking, self expression and self discipline. Children should be trained to resolve their quarrels and conflicts with their peers in a peaceful manner instead of physical fighing and violent means.

Children at secondary stage are sensitive to grasp the informations healthy or unhealthy from media, newspapers and internet etc., hence they should be helped to decide what is wrong and what is right. This is the beginning of the age of idealism. Teachers can complement this tendency by getting them think about the kind of world they want to live in. Curriculum at this stage should be designed to develop in children informed aversion to various types of violence in the society as, communal fighting, gender discrimination and discrimination

A Education for peace must begin with our everyday experiences and immediate fears, not with more models of peaceful world order or of a peaceful social life.

Hans Nicklas And Anne Osterman (The Psychology of Deterrence and the Chances for Education in Peace)-

on the basis of caste, class, religion, region and language etc. A sense of maturity may be developed to respond to various types of corruptions, bribery, dishonesty and other malacious activities pervading in the society. Teachers can stress the contributions of great people like Mahatma Gandhi, Raja Ram Mohan Roy, Dr. Martin Luthurking Jr, Abraham Lincoln and others who dedicated their lives to peace and justice. Students can be motivated to devote their lives to humanitarian causes.

Senior Secondary Stage

This is the period of adolescence when pupils grow from puberty to adulthood. Erikson identified adolescence as a crisis of identity versus role confusion.[21] Identity confusion may result in impulsive or poorly thought-out actions. The young students at this stage are concerned about their identity and are conscious about how they appear to others. Though they are not mature, but they want to be free and independent from the protective enclosure of their parents and elders. Out of confusion and conflicts, they use to fight and quarrel with their parents, peers and teachers.

Adolescence age is a tender stage of life as far as emotional development is concerned. At this stage skills for rational thinking, self expression, self discipline and communication should be reinforced. The student should be trained to resolve their conflicts in day to day life through dialogue or negotiation. They should be made aware of the issues related to the problems of population growth, environmental destruction and other moral maladies of life in modern civil society. Teachers should

It is now imperative that we will grow up become adults, and learn to use this magnificent democracy which we are all anxious to preserve. We are not children and the "experts" are not our benevolent parents who have our best interests at heart.

David P. Barash and Judith Eve Lipton (Stop Nuclear War)

make young students understand the inter-relationship and mutual dependence in the global and ecological perspective so that they could form their attitudes towards peace and non-violence. They should be motivated to examine the existing social, political and economic systems at national and international levels. In the present time of turbulence in the whole world, our adolescents are facing a difficult era when they are insecure, they have got lots of tensions, anxieties and worries about their career and blurred future. Hence in the curriculum, there should be provisions for counseling, guidance, yoga and meditation so as to make them emotionally balanced and peaceful persons.

Today apart from various types of tensions and anxieties regarding insecure future, adolescence is also at great risk, because young students in this period are vulnerable to various influences of negative and evil forces that emerge from the techno-scientific progress and permissiveness in the present society. They are living on the 'edge', from where they can either be directed to pursue the right path to honourable life, or they can be allowed to follow the path of anti social life. Hence, the curricula at senior secondary stage should be designed and its transactional process be organised in such a way so that adolescents are protected from the blows of 'evils' in the present world. The education at this stage needs support of home and the society as well.

Higher Education Stage

As far as higher education is concerned, it is the most important period for youths are the greatest asset of any society or of the world in the larger context. The Universities and other institutions of higher education are the powerhouses where tremendous energy of youth may be explored and channelised

This is education as stuffing the brain and not training the mind.

Swami Vivekananda-

to improve the world. Through carefully designed curricula combined with teaching methodologies a Culture of Peace may be promoted in and outside the campuses of universities and schools. Today, youths are living in a violent and permissive society. A philosophy of permissiveness which invaded throughout the developed world like U.S.A, Australia etc. has now entered the eastern nations. This philosophy combined with terror and violence is destroying the soul of people concerned and also destroying their happiness and peace; consequently sex, violence and all types of malpractices are creeping in our societies. These are the 'evils' of modern society which are afflicting human civilisation today. During such a decline, it is the youth that are adversely affected most. Today youths are afflicted with the craze for organic cravings and satisfactions unchecked and undisciplined. They seek only pleasure. Thus, sheer pursuit of unchecked individual pleasure uninspired by any standard of ethical and moral values has lowered down the quality of human life and human taste.[22] It has ruined the family bonds, social ethics and the whole civilisation. The unchecked tendencies of people have created chaos and turbulence in the present world.

Thus, in designing the curricula at higher education stage, the present state of world should be taken into account, where youths are suffering from maladies of the modern permissive society. They are suffering from psychic and personality distortions that are being manifested through their obnoxious activities as violence, destruction, murder, rape, depression and suicides in the campuses of educational institutions. Other than moral decline, the present world is facing thunderous blows of terrorism from time to time. Recently, India and the world have

To facilitate education for justice and peace, one must above all believe: believe that justice and peace are possible, believe that each and everyone of us can do something to bring justice and peace into being.

Diag. C. James (Reflections on Education for Justice and Peace)-

witnessed two incidence of awful terrorism, one in New York, America (9/11) and another is Mumbai, India. (26/11). These incidences of terrorism have shaken the whole world and created a war like situation. Hence, at this point of human history, higher education has to take major stake in the process of promoting peace in the world.

In this respect, two conferences on higher education may be rightly mentioned: one the UNESCO World Conference on Higher Education in Paris (October 1998) and other, Conference on Higher Education for Peace in Tromso, Norway held on 4-6 May, 2000. Both the Conferences respectively aimed to challenge the higher education institutions on their role as peace builders and promoters of culture of peace.

Tromso Conference acclaimed that there is a great need to fill the gap between theory and practice at the higher education stage. Today the task of higher education is to seek solutions to issues of, ***'how the peace aspects might be focused on in higher education.*** The contents and methodology of peace education, focusing in particular on higher education and its impact on the whole field of education-formal and non formal, from universities to day care centres and communities, should be explored from various angles.

The Conference further acclaimed that the task of higher education is to seek the solution of ***"How might syllabuses, pedagogy, organisation and evaluation in higher education affect the notion of peace and conflict-transformation in civil societies and states. How peace education teaching programme might challenge the traditional divide between theory and practice in the institutions of higher education."***[23]

The Conference suggested that, since both conflict and act of peace are based on human relations, hence 'peace building' should be constituted as a practical discipline in the higher education. The experience of practical peace building should be transformed in the humanities, and sciences of nature. The Conference felt that, another great challenge to higher education is to develop innovative and creative methods of education, which enable and motivate the students to take part in practical peace efforts.[24]

Moreover, curriculum development in higher education may follow the ideas of Hague Appeal for Peace: Global Campaign for Peace Education, (1998) that is, "A culture of peace will be achieved when citizens of the world understand global problems, have the skills to resolve conflicts and struggle for justice non-violently, live by international standards of human rights and equity, appreciate cultural diversity and respect the Earth and each other. Such learning can only be achieved with systematic education for peace".

Thus, while shaping higher education to develop the culture of peace, various peace concepts as, understanding of global problems, skills of conflict resolution, non-violent struggle for justice, human rights and equity in the context of the nation and the world, appreciation of cultural diversity, respect for Earth and it's eco-system and mutual respect in human beings might be integrated with the existing traditional curriculum of almost all subjects in higher education, including engineering, technology and medical science. The research results of various institutions concerned with peace studies and peace researches at national and international level should be properly communicated to students through well organised curriculum. The students should have every opportunity to practice and participate in conflict resolution and peace building processes at local, national and at the world level.

Today, it is a great matter of concern that higher education curriculum should be inclined not only towards the global market and attainment of organic pleasure but towards the spiritual development of youth. Higher education must play a role of safety guard that could check our youth from becoming morally sick, anti-socials and terrorists in extreme cases.

In India particularly, we have a large population of youths, so there is a large amount of youth power that may be used as an asset for the nation. The energies of youth should not be wasted in wrong hands and in wrong directions rather that should be channelised to promote peace in the world in larger context. Hence at the level of higher education, knowledge, experience and dreams should be combined in such away so as to change the Culture of War to Culture of Peace.[25]

Contents of Adult Education for Peace

Throughout the world, much of the work on Education for Peace has been carried out in the area of school education – elementary and secondary schools. Adult education for peace is the less focused area as far as research and studies on peace are concerned, though adult education for peace is more important for all people who are responsible for peace issues outside the periphery of schools and colleges.

Unless adults including parents and community people engage in activities to create peace in their families and community, how can we expect that the new generation will be peaceful and will further create a peaceful society. The importance of adult education for peace increased since the Malta Agreement between USA and USSR in 1989.[26] Afterwards United Nation declared 1994 as the "International Year of the Family"

The future is in hands of those who an give tomorrow's generations valid reasons to live and to hope. The message of the Aquariums Conspiracy is that there is ripeness for a Yes.

Marilyn Ferguson (The Aquarian Conspiracy Personal and Social Transformation):-

and recognised the educational roles of parents and other adults toward children significant.

UN acclaimed that parents can educate their children to create both, conflicts and friendly relationships among nations. Furthermore the influence of education by parents are much greater than those provided by schools. The earnest efforts of teachers in teaching peace to children may be less effective if parents teach the affirmation of violence. The need for adult education for peace is easily understandable if we consider the effects of parents as educators.[27]

The United Nations Conventions on the Rights of the Child was held on 20th November 1989 and was effective from September 1990, and dealt with the child specific needs and rights. The Convention acknowledged that every child has certain basic rights, including the right to life, his or her own name and identity, to be raised by his or her parents within a family or cultural grouping and have relationship with their parents, even if they are seperated.

The Convention obliged states to allow parents to exercise their parental responsibilities. It also acknowledged that children have the right to express their opinions and to have those opinions heard and acted upon when appropriated, to be protected from abuse or exploitation, to have their privacy protected and requires that their lives not be subjected to excessive interference.[28] Today it is matter of great concern that, how can obligations of the Convention be fulfilled and the rights of children be secured fully in the absence of properly designed and well directed adult education programmes at national and international levels.

In general adult education is less controlled than formal education. Specially in India, the status of adult education is not very distinct rather blurred after more than six decades of independence. As far as implementation of adult education is concerned, ground realities are far apart from policies of governments. Adult education is facing severe problems regarding interests of adult learners, relevancy of curriculum, availability of adult literature and text books, training of adult educators, commitment of teachers and personnel, adequate funds and infrastructure and last not the least indifferent attitudes of ministries and governments. Mostly NGOs are involved in adult education in their own capacities. In this way, adult education is being carried out half heartedly in India, perhaps the status may be same in other parts of the world also.

In this situation how can we expect that such a large population of adults will be educated for Peace and Parenthood from the perspective of the UN Convention on the Child. However adult education for peace is imperative in the present context of the world which is facing challanges of war, violence, terrorism, exploitations, environmental destruction and various types of agitations nationally and internationally. In the present perspective adult education for peace should be rather treated as lifelong education. In the democratic set up of a nation, adults have full right as citizen, which enable them to decide national policies and to change political trends internationally. Adults with such rights have more significant roles to play in creating a peaceful world. Hence they should be inevitably educated for peace building, first in their homes and next in communities and society.

Bon Ki Moon, Secretary General of the United Nations in his speech to General Assembly on October 13th 2006, addressed to adult educators that, ***"understanding and respect as well as acceptance of cultural variety must be at the foundation***

of one's relationship to all others. When prejudice, discrimination and racism are expressed, adult education should take responsibility for opposing any such views."[29] Moon's statement implies that, adults should be educated to understand, respect and accept the cultural diversity so as to make the mutual relationships for harmonious living.

David Silvera in his article, "Conflict Resolutions, Human Rights and Adult Education", emphasised 'Mediation' as a tool of conflict resolution and suggested that, ***"The process of Mediation in conflict resolution, human rights and achieving peace can be recognised as part of the Universal Principle of Adult Education."***[30]

Charles B. Paraselle in his article, "Mediators as International Peacemakers" considered, language as a criteria for distinction between humans and animals, between violence and non-violence. He wrote in his article ***"Animals do not misunderstand each other as much as we do. If, as seems likely, connection exists between language and violence, than consideration of language has place in the field of conflict resolution."***[31] Thus 'mediation' is one of the methods of Alternative Conflict Resolution (ACR). It is a tool in human relations, negotiations and conflict resolution because it exposes the hidden interests in a relationship, tries to give an answer to what is important and not to the statements made.[32] In negotiation, we have to change the attitude of people involved from competition and confrontation to collaboration.

As a philosophy 'Mediation' believes in dialogue and not in antagonism, adversary or violence. According to the Americans, Jay Folbery and Alison Taylor in their book 'Mediation', ***"mediation is an intervention that is intended to resolve dispute and manage conflict by facilitating decision making."***[33]

Mediation has definite stages involving a series of techniques for accomplishing necessary tasks, which one can learn by training that involves one's personal life experience, theoretical lectures and role play in story and real conflicts.[34]

Hence in the light of the suggestions by Davil Silvera (mediator and trainer of mediation) and others, Adult Education must include in addition to existing curricula, the following subjects (theory and practical) as:

- training of skills of language
- training of the technique of mediation
- theoretical lectures on Children's Right (mentioned in the Convention on the Children's Right) and Child Psychology
- to make the adult learners understand the issues of war, violence, terrorism, exploitation, environmental destruction, their causes and remedies.
- training for citizenship so that they could know their rights and duties, national policies, political trends at national and international level.

Other than aforesaid contents of curriculum for Adult Education for Peace, we can take into account the non-violent methods of peace-making and conflicts resolutions used by Mahatma Gandhi in his serious and long continuing efforts to develop training programmes to help people prepare for non-violent struggle during freedom fight in India. To a world used to the incentives of greed and fear, Gandhi gave an alternative, the driving force of love. Gandhi called his new tool 'Satyagraha', which literally meant insistence upon or adherence to truth,[35] but he described Satyagraha as a way of life. Satyagraha has a creed, a value system and certain methods of working. Gandhi practiced Satyagraha as an art and used it as a means of conflict resolution and protest against the hostile actions of enimies or authorities. Satyagraha has different phases of actions by people:

- Self preparation
- Revolution at home
- Learning from the people
- Loving the people
- Mass organisation
- Constructive work
- Small scale laboratories
- Direct action

Gandhi emphasised the training of people for self preparation, that is the development of inner faculties through study, inner search and meditation. This is the inner work of personal growth and transformation. Social change is brought through reforms, legislation, revolution etc. This is the outer work of Satyagraha.

According to Gandhi, revolution begins at home, hence people must be motivated to develop the spirit of community living in their home through activities as:

- Enjoying together
- Suffering together
- Praying together

At the community level, people should be involved in:

- Community prayer
- Community sanitation

To Gandhi Satyagraha was much more than a non- violent teachique: it was an educational process that would not only create among the satya grahis an acute awareness of injustice and exploitation, but also restore their dignity and self respect.

Amrut W. Nakhre (Peace Action as Peace Education: An Analysis of the Impact of Satyagraha on Participants)-

- Group study
- Celebrating festivals

In the economic field Satyagraha lays stress on dignity of labour and non-ownership of land and property. In the political field Satyagraha lays stress on eschewing power and taking care of means because means should be pure for means predict ends. In the educational field Satyagraha tries to strike at the root of the existing system by introducing alternative education. Satyagrah further suggests steps for non-violent direct actions. Hence people must be trained to take action as,

- Identify injustice
- Understand the adversary
- Communicate with opponent
- Educate public opinion
- Procession
- Non-violent non-cooperation
- Civil Disobedience
- Non violent interventions
- Training
- Arbitration, Mediation, Adjudication
- Creating parallel structures.[36]

Thus Satyagraha seems to be an appropriate tool to resist, protest and oppose the dictum of authorities. It is a tool of conflict resolution, arbitration, mediation and lastly the building of peace. Hence 'Satyagraha' may be included as practical discipline in Adult Education.

Only the people or communities trained in such components of 'peace building' can provide conducive environment to coming generation to grow as peace oriented citizens of the world.

Text book writing

Text book writing is the next foremost step after the development of curriculum from elementary stage to higher education and adult education. Text books convey attitudes and values explicitly and implicitly. Every aspect of text books- language, contents and presentation including illustrations tend to either a pro-peace or pro-violence treatment. It is therefore important to ensure that text books are written and designed from the perspective of education for peace.[37]

Ideally textbook writing should take into account the larger context in which personality development of child takes place. Authors should be aware of the serious issues regarding environmental destruction, population growth, moral decline of the society, cultural diversities, socio-economic inequalities, exploitations, discriminations and prejudices based on caste, creed and gender prevalent in the society. Moreover, emerging peace issues as war, violence and terrorism throughout the world should be considered while writing text books. Not only this, lessons designed in the text books must highlight the current issues, problems, conflicts and conflict resolutions and peace efforts of the past and present. Authors should take precautions while treating sensitive issues like religion and beliefs of particular communities. They should be neutral and honest in the treatment of subjects as history and social sciences.

As far as peace issues are concerned, they may be infused with the existing contents of text books so as to reinforce the efforts of teachers in communicating peace messages to children in their classrooms. Every subject pertaining to natural sciences, social sciences and humanities have sufficient base and space for the infusion of peace elements. Only precautions should be taken in the selection of materials for, it must be appropriate for the age and level of students. Authors must have creative powers to infuse various peace elements into existing course.

For the infusion, existing text books at elementary, secondary and higher education should be properly reviewed and examined from peace perspective and then it should be seen where peace, justice, human rights and other peace values can be infused. Text books must provide instructional strategies which may help teachers to adjust the contents to the abilities, needs and interests of students.

In India, after analysing and reviewing the text books at primary education level, PROBE Report has shown various anomalies in the writing of text books. These anomalies pertain to the issues of scheduled caste, untouchable communities, women and their subordination, sex stereotyping, poverty and other issues. Hence NCERT (2005) suggested: "Every text books must be thoroughly and critically reviewed for its contents, treatment, and overall vision....... Attention needs to be paid to the language used in textbooks so as to ensure that their sensibility is conducive to nurturing courteous, aesthetically sensitive and socially aware human beings.[38] Text books, in the end are as good as their fate in hands of teachers. Here it is to be noted that, only by infusing peace issues and values in textbooks nothing is going to happen unless these lessons are taught in a fashion that could be effective enough to form the personality of students by significant change in the attitude and skills. Therefore pedagogy is supposed to be the core of all essential strategies of Education for Peace. The success of Education for Peace implies a commitment not only to certain educational contents but to a pedagogy that gives teachers and students an opportunity to practice some of the essential values pertaining to peace, that Education for Peace is concerned about transmitting. Thus Education for Peace does not rely on the conventional teaching of concepts and events presented in text books rather it is the concretisation of peace values into action. Its transactional process is the core of all strategies and planning of imparting it.

Pedagogy of Education for Peace

In general, pedagogic goal for teachers is syllabus and examination oriented but teaching methodologies for Education for Peace focus not merely on memorisation of texts, retention of concepts, or achieving individual goals in examinations and competitions rather on learning to reflect, share, care and collaborate with each other. The methods of teaching should be creative, child-centred, largly experimental and participatory. The pedagogy of Education for Peace include the creation of suitable learning experiences, discussions, debate, presentation, group and cooperative projects depending on students maturity levels and the subject contents. The pedagogic approach to Education for Peace is stage-specific and context-specific, hence the appropriate strategies should be devised to develop among students (at various stages of education) a sense of open mindedness and comprehension about cultural diversities, historical events, human affairs and fundamental values of life. There is sufficient room in the syllabi of various subject areas for teaching students problem solving, conflict resolution by adopting peaceful means and eschewing violence. Thus, teachers need to take advantage of this. They can use strategies like encouraging Enquiry, question-answers, experiments, discussions, dialogues, value clarification, jurisprudential model, story telling, anecdotes, games, examples setting, analogies, metaphors, role play and simulation. There are examples of pedagogic strategies which can be tried out as per requirement in various contexts and at different stages of education. These are as follows:

The Enquiry Method

The enquiry method of teaching does not rely on memorisation of texts rather it stresses the importance of

All that we are is the result of what we have thought.

Buddha-

experience in solving a problem and arriving at guaranteed solution. This methodology is a teaching style where students with minimum guidance of teacher seek out to discover and create a solution to a recognised problem through procedure of enquiry. This method is also called problem solving or discovery approach. The procedure involves the steps as: defining the problem, developing a tentative solution or construction of hypothesis, collecting and classifying the available data, testing against new evidences and generalising the results.

The enquiry method is process oriented rather than context oriented; it is conceptual as well as factual it is student centred rather than teacher centred. This method develops among students critical thinking and favourable attitude towards the subject matter, but it needs the support and supervision of teacher and institutional authorities.

- ***Value Clarification Approach***

In various subjects there are many controversial topics which present value-laden issues. These can be best dealt with the teaching methodology called Value Clarification Approach. Under this approach, students and teachers actively engage in the formulation and examination of values. This method does not teach a set of values rather it involves the students in practical experiences, making them aware of their own feelings, ideas, opinions, beliefs and attitudes, so that the choices and decisions they make are conscious and deliberate and are based on their own value system,

This methodology is being used to deal with the topics like ethnic killing, social behaviour, moral dilemma, war, defence expenditure, literacy and poverty alleviation programmes etc.

- ***Jurisprudential model of teaching***

This model is used to teach a Moral Dilemma which consists of four steps:

1. Confront a moral dilemma,
2. State a position on the original or alternative moral dilemma,
3. Testing the reasoning for a position on a moral dilemma; and
4. Reflect on a reason for the position.

In this strategy, students are asked to describe their perception freely about the central figure or message in a story or poetry or articles and they are asked to tell, how they could feel in similar situation.[39]

- ***Role Playing***

In this approach, students explore human relations and problems by enacting problem situations. In role playing, they can explore feelings, attitudes, values and problem solving methods. Role playing is a model of teaching which has roots in both, in individual and social dimensions of education. This method allows individuals to work together in analysing social situations and interpersonal problems. The role playing involves the participants and observers in real problem situation and helps them to find solutions for their own problems.

- ***Dramatics and Literary Activities***

Dramatics is very interesting way to motivate students for carrying out activities related to Education for Peace. Some of the peace issues like terrorism and violence can be dramatised to sensitise students towards these major issues. Besides, literary activities like songs, pictures, paintings, drawings and shows can be arranged by consulting relevant literatures, books, case studies etc. Through these activities, various issues regarding violation of peace may be highlighted and student's reaction can be obtained for restoration of peace.

- ***Social Service Camps***

To get real feeling of peace and direct experiences, social service camps can be organised in those areas where peace has been disturbed by violence and terrorism. Students should make people aware of consequences of violence and pursue them to live together with peace and harmony. This strategy may be used at the higher education level where students can be motivated to use their energies and enthusiasm to change the world. The youths through social service camps can help those deprived people who are not provided their legitimate dues. At the university level, through NSS (National Service Scheme) and social service camps young students may undertake field work related to upliftment of children of weaker section and other peace issues.

- ***Multi-Media Approach***

For imparting education for peace, multimedia approach that can be suitably used, include the media as: printed media (books, newspapers, journals, charts, posters, comics, photographic stories and novels etc.) radio, television, satellite communication systems, internet, website, films, documentaries, tape recorders, CDs, theatres, folk media (street plays, folk theater, folk dance and folk songs, folk tales) and puppet shows etc.

- ***Ideographic Approach***

Field workers have developed unique methods to educate the masses. These methods are called Ideographic Approach. Peace corps workers are using these methods as per requirements. Ideographic approach includes: field survey, demonstrations, talks of experts, panel discussion, symposia, debates, games, case studies, group discussions brain storming sessions, attitudes mapping, desensitisation seminars, contests and quiz.

Other than these methods there are various means for acquiring inner peace:

- ***Introspection***

The individual introspects himself and becomes aware of his strengths and weaknesses. He becomes the observer of his own internal conflicts and he finds out the cause of the same. This process leads to self awakening and self improvement. Introspection is an appropriate method of educating youths and adults to prepare for peace.

Gandhi's method of Satyagraha to resolve conflict and protest against authorities starts from self preparation which includes introspection as its first step. J. Krishnamurti's method of transformation of an individual to a peaceful person requires self knowledge. Obviously introspection must be an imperative process inclusion in knowing oneself.

Yoga and Meditation

Yoga in the perspective of Education for Peace should be practical Yoga, which is extensively being practiced all over the world. For common men and students the techniques of Yoga includes physical purification (Shatkarma) physical exercises or postures (Asanas) and breathing exercises (Paranayam) which are easy to practice. The Yoga with its emphasis on muscular discipline and respiratory control promotes health and strength and automatically stimulates the latent power of the mind. Students may be trained to practice Yogic exercises to attain the conditions of meditation. Yoga is the science of body, mind and intellect and is a powerful instrument to keep the emotions balanced in this chaotic and violence ridden world.

Institutional Climate

The congenial and peaceful institutional climate provide for the promotion of peace. Every person concerned should try his best to promote and propagate peace. This includes equity to all the seniors and juniors, autonomy of thought and expression and co-operation in planning and execution the inter-relationship between head and the staff, between head and

Spiritual energy brings compassion into the world.

Christina Balwin-

students, teachers and their colleagues and other staffs, teachers and their students, should be that of acceptance, tolerance, openness and respect. This type of relationship contributes in making the environment congenial for the promotion of peace.

- ***Morning Assembly***

Morning assembly is the common ritual in schools, but school authorities and teachers should try to integrate the activities of morning assembly with the ideals or values, it is meant to transact. It should not be mere recital of verses. The students should be able to internalise the real meaning of feeling of calm, quiet and peacefulness. In the morning assembly, thought for the day can be presented to stir the thoughts of the students and may inspire them to do a bit for achieving higher ideals like, tolerance, co-operation, peace etc.

- ***Games and Sports***

The students should be given maximum opportunity for games and sports to be fit. Only a healthy and fit person can withstand and cope the challenges and stress of the modern life and the fast competitive world. Various emotions as aggression, adventures find outlet in a socially approved way. Games provide satisfaction, tranquility and relaxation of mind to students. The physical games and sports provide them positive energy to do mental work.

- ***Counselling***

The students need counselling in the educational premises where they have to deal with violent, aggressive and morally and emotionally critical situations. Now a days they need counselling badly because they are vulnerable to violence, depression and suicidal tendencies in the high pace moving world.

- ***Teaching of Regular Subjects***

Various subjects and course contents should not be taught in segregation rather teaching of these subjects should be made meaniful in the perspective of the current problems the world or human society is facing. For example, if a teacher is teaching nuclear fission or fusion in Physics, he should highlight its uses for the welfare of mankind and the destruction it will bring when misused. While teaching History, a teacher can emphasise the destruction and catastrophe of wars which people fought to achieve nothing. In the subjects like Social Studies, Civics, Economics, teachers can highlight the issues related to human relations, democracy, cause of poverty and its alleviations, and so on and so forth. In the subjects like Botany and Zoology a teacher may raise the issue of eco-balance and environmental protection, Similarly in other subjects which are concerned with the cognition and emotional development as Psychology and Education teachers may deliberately throw light on the issues which can affect the minds of students positively.

- ***Time Management***

In the high pace world students from the initial period of education should be trained to manage their time. They should be made aware that time in the modern perspective is very important and valuable so they should know how to manage time to achieve their goal. If a person does not know the management of time, he is going to fail in the modern perspective. Hence, students should be trained to organise their day to day routine to achieve maximum.

Other than, aforestated pedagogical means or ways, of giving Education for Peace there are several other methods like, tours, travels, cultural exchange, hobby classes, celebrations of national festivals, religious festivals, international festivals, celebrations of the birth anniversaries of great persons etc which can contribute in developing the feelings of mutual appreciation and tolerance among students.

References

1. Harris, Ian, M. (1998) *Peace Education* London, Mc Farland & Company, Inc. Publishers, p. 14.

2. Betty Reardon (1982) *Militarization, Security and Peace Education: A Guide for Concerned Citizens* Valley Forge PA: United Ministries in Education, pp. 16-17.

3. NCERT (2006) *National Curriculum Frame work, 2005. Position Paper, National Focus Group on Education for Peace*. New Delhi, NCERT.

4. UNESCO (1995). *UNESCO and a Culture of Peace* UNESCO publishing www.unesco.orgcpp/UK/news.html.

5. Declaration and Programme of Action for a Culture of Peace, adopted by the UN General Assembly (1999)http//www. Unesco.Org/cpp/UK/declaration/ 2000tm

6. The Hague Agenda for Peace and Justice for 21st Century, UN Document: Ref A/54/98 www.un/prg/cyberschool bus/peace

7. *Ibid.*

8. UNICEF (1999). Peace Education in UNICEF. Working Paper Series, July 1999.

9. NCERT (2006) op. cit., p. 1.

10. Harris op.cit., p. 7.

11. *Ibid.*, p. 38.

12. Boulding E (1975). *The Personhood of Children* (Philadelphia PA: Religious Education Committee, Friends General Conference) p. 13.

13. Harris, op cit., p. 145.

14. James and Mc. Ginnis, K (1983), *Parenting for Peace and Justice*. Maryknoll N.Y. Orbis Books, p. 37.

15. Harris, op.cit., p. 145.

16. Jersild, A.T. (1935) "Children's Fears", *Child Development Monograph.*

17. Harris, *ibid.* p. 149.

18. Educational Policy Commission & National Education Associates (1943), Education and the People's peace, Washington D.C.

19. Harris, op. cit., p. 150.

20. Tourney, J.V. (1947) *Political Socialization Research in United States, Handbook on Peace Education.* ed. Christoph Wulf Frank furt, International Peace Research Association.

21. Erikson E. (1968) *Identity: Youth and Crisis*, New York Norton.

22. Ranganathananda (1986) *Eternal Values for a Changing Society, Education for Human Excellence,* Vol. II, Bombay, Bhartiya Vidya Bhavan, pp. 368-369.

23. Mjos, Ole. D. (2000) Higher Education for Peace, a paper contributed in conference in Tromso, Norway http//www. peacw2uit. no/hefp/ contribution/paper

24. *Ibid.*

25. *Ibid.*

26. Fujita Hideo (1995) *Adult Education for Peace: Japnese Experience.* Lund University Sweden, R&D Group, School of Education http//www/eric.ed.gov /Eric Web Portal.

27. *Ibid.*

28. Convention on the Rights of the Child, from Wikipedia original text. http//enwikipedia.org/wik/convention on the Rights of child.

29. Silvera, David (2006) Conflict Resolution, Human Rights and Adult Education www.eaea.org/doc/members/kenya full paper-ICAE.

30. *Ibid.*

31. *Ibid.*

32. *Ibid.*

33. *Ibid.*

34. *Ibid.*

35. Knaebel, jeff 92008). Note on Satyagraha, *Mahatma Gandhi Community Forum* http//www/gandhi serve.org/message-board/

36. *Ibid.*

37. NCERT (2005) National Curriculum Framework, Position paper, National Focus Group on Education for Peace,_New Delhi, NCERT (2006) p. 20.

38. *Ibid.*, p. 21.

39. Mavi, N.S. (2004), Instructional Paradigms for Imparting Education for Peace, paper contributed in Seminar. On Education for Peace, Our Main Priority 5th March 2004. Ludhiana, Malwa Central College of Education for Women.

6

Teacher: A Role Model

Education for Peace is an ideal endeavor that can only be carried out in an ideal environment imbued with culture of peace. Today it is an unfortunate fact that our educational institutions are a part and parcel of the society (may be Indian or the world) that is oriented towards culture of war and terrorism rather than culture of peace. These institutions do not function in isolation rather in the framework of society that is in turbulence, they are catered by the groups of people who belong to such society. Teachers, students, office bearers, heads of the institutions and departments and other functionaries, all come from every nook and corner of such society. Hence, educational process and environment of educational institutions as schools, colleges and universities are highly inflicted and pressed by turbulence in the surrounding society and the world in larger context.

The only league of Nations that gives any assurance of permanent peace is the league which teachers of the earth shall write in the minds and hearts of children

Education and the Peoples Peace (1943), Washington D.C.

As far as Education for Peace in India is concerned, it is a matter of great consideration that, who will operationalise and implement such type of education? Who will translate such education into reality?

Literally almost all sections of people who are associated with the educational system and responsible for the operationalisation of education for peace, belong to such a society which is declining morally day by day. However, it is an inevitable fact that teacher is the 'core' of educational enterprise, hence he can't get rid of his responsibility and the role assigned to him to carry the Education for Peace in the realm of class-rooms.

Today if the world is inclined to seek a long term means to build and promote peace on this planet earth, we have to opt for education and ultimately we should go for teachers as they will contribute by performing their role in building and promoting culture of peace among children and in their institutional environment that will further extend peace to the community, society, nation and lastly to the world.

The assigned role of teacher has background of thousand years of human history where teachers played the role of helms men in the process of social and political change.

Teacher a Role Model: Historical Background

There are various examples in world history which show, how teachers had been the role models to their students such as Greek educators and thinkers like Plato and Aristotle. Plato was the student of Socrates and Aristotle was the student of Plato. Teachers and taughts both, were the great philosophers and educational thinkers whose thoughts even today, flow in the present world to direct the societies. Aristotle was the great teacher who taught Alexander the Great. Trever in 'History of

Ancient Civilization' has written; ***"Rarely have two such master spirits been associated as teacher and pupil."***[1] He further wrote, ***"Alexander may well have learned from him the virtues of moderation and self mastery, regard for reason, the disinterested love of knowledge and the theory and practice of politics,"***[2] In eighteenth century Europe Pestalozzi and Herbart were such educators, Herbart joined the school of Pestalozzi in his later age to have practical experience of the educational philosophies of Pestalozzi. Pestalozzi said, ***"That is the greatest praise you can give me. I have succeeded, thank God, in showing the world that there must be no gulf between the home and school."***[3]

There are several more examples of teacher-pupil relationships in the history of mankind. In ancient Vedic period of India the teacher was expected not only to impart information and skills but lead and guide his students to 'supreme knowledge'. He was 'Guru' which means great in learning and moral conduct. He was called Acharya which comes from the word 'Car' (to behave) and means one who trains up others in good behaviour (âcâram grähayati iti äcäryah): it is also taken by some to mean the source of all religion (dharmän äcinoti iti äcäryah). In other sense, the teacher was expected to train the pupils in good behaviour - the essence of religion and naturally to possess those qualities himself. Teacher was not only the one who passed on only 'inert ideas' to his pupils but he had the ability to explain, expound, expand and re-interpret the knowledge in the light of his own experiences.[4] Hence Indian teacher was the guide, leader, creator and disseminator of knowledge with high moral character and was recognised as a role-model for students to follow him. In the Vedic Gurukula system of education, teaching-learning environment was kept imbued with the culture of peace by invoking blessings of God by peace chants (Santi Patha) before the discourses of Guru or Acharya. The acharyas or teachers usually maintained high ideals of life themselves to build and promote culture of peace in their own institutions of learning and the society alike.

In Vedic period, teacher enjoyed a special status and position, he was held in high esteem by the society not only due to his learning and scholarship but also due to qualities of head, heart and hands. The Guru or the teacher was an embodiment of good qualities, a fountain of knowledge and abode of spirituality.[5]

Here is a great example of teacher who was the real mentor of his disciple, he was Chanakya or Kautilya. Chanakya was the teacher of Prince Chandragupta. He was primarily concerned with the education of the prince but he prescribed the entire circle of knowledge – social, philosophical, economic and political being made up of Anvikshiki, Trayi and Dandaniti. He also prescribed the companionship of a man of ripe wisdom and culture for his disciple (prince) as the root of mental and moral growth. Kautilya was always there (as a prime minister in the court of emperor Chandragupta) to help him to carry Maurya Dynasty for a long period.[6] Kautilya is an example of a teacher who caused a great social and political change through his wisdom and ideas. He got released the subjects from the misrule of Nanda Dynasty by teaching and grooming his disciple, who further rooted out the Nanda Dynasty completely.

Not very unlike the ancient Indian period during medieval times also teachers were a respectable class. The 'Ulemas' devoted their entire life for learning and teaching. They were called Ulama-i-akharat.[7]During the reign of Akbar, teaching was recognised such a respectable and auspicious occupation that the scholars and learned men were called from far and wide. The learned teachers from Arabia, Persia and Bokhara were invited to teach in Agra University, a great seat of learning. There is strong evidence to suggest that in medieval period, the reputed theologians and scholars who earned name and fame by the scholarly works were appointed teachers in Madarsas and Maktabs.[8]

History shows that, the teacher enjoyed respect and reverence from ancient times till the arrival of Britishers in India. By eighteenth century after Renaissance in Europe, things changed very fast with the advancement of science and technology, new subjects of knowledge drew attention of leaders and thinkers. With the arrival of East India Company and subsequently the British government, the form of education took a new direction. With the advent of formal system of education, teacher's role became formal but still then good and scholarly teachers used to receive respect. The teachers training institutions were established to enhance the qualities and professionalism in teachers. The main aim of teachers training was, to prepare them for imparting education according to Britisher's need.

During freedom struggle and political turmoil in India, great teachers and educational thinkers emerged with their educational thoughts and institutions as, Swami Vivekananda, Tagore, Gandhi, Pandit Madan Mohan Malviya, Aurobindo, Annie Besant, J. Krishnamurti, Sir Syed Ahmed Khan, Radhakrishnan, Zakir Hussain and so forth. They provided models to establish and promote education in India as per the needs of Indian soil. In the galaxy of renowned teachers J. Krishnamurti (or Jiddu Krishnamurti) claimed allegiance to no nationality, caste, religion or philosophy and spent his life traveling the world as an individual speaker, speaking to large and small groups, as well as with interested individuals. He authored a number of books, among them are, The First and Last Freedom, The only Revolution and Kishnamurti's Note Book. There is a large collection of his talks and discussions which have been published, among them 'You are The World' is most popular and famous collection of his talks. At the age of

90, he addressed the United Nations on the subject of peace and awareness and was awarded the 1984 Peace Medal.[9] Perhaps, one can say, all these teachers were exceptions and had superman qualities but it was the fact that, it was the period, till good and scholarly teachers in general, due to their high moral character got respect in society and played the role model for their students. But with passage of time, teacher's role seemingly became insignificant rather diluted and presently it seems to be faded out. This has become a matter of worry and anxiety specially in the perspective of Education for Peace, which mainly relies on the shoulders of teachers. Realising the role of teacher in the whole teaching-learning process, Kothari Commission (1964-66) enunciated, ***"No system of education can rise above the level of its teachers. No matter how well the policies are formulated, in the ultimate analysis it is the teacher who implements it in the class-room situations.[10]*** Further, National Policy of Education (NPE, 1986) and its revised version NPE (1992) recommended that, ***"The Government and the community should endeavour to create conditions which will help, motivate and inspire teachers on constructive and creative lines, to device appropriate methods of communications and activities relevant to the needs and capabilities of and concerns of the community.[11]***

The Teacher Education Curriculum Framework (1978) revised in 1988, accepted the role of teacher as an agent of social transformation and believed that, "in order to be a catalyst in the process of developing a citizen who is productive, believe in justice and national integration and possesses values befitting a democratic socialist and secular society, the teacher himself needs to become such a citizen through appropriate learning experiences.

Thus emphasising on the training of teachers in the pedagogical theories, the Framework therefore suggested that,

"the pedagogical theory should create awareness among the student-teachers of national scene and sharpen their social sensitivity which in turn have similar impact on children. Such social sensitivity is key to ensuring peace and harmony in the society. The student teachers should be exposed to real situations with the programme on working with community".[12] It was hoped that, the programme will provide an opportunity for interaction among teachers and various sections of the society. It exposes them to often conflicting situations and helps them to appreciate the social dynamics and pluralistic sensitivity.

The Curriculum Framework for Quality Teacher Education (1998) brought out by NCTE (National council of Teacher Education) addressed, the diversities prevailing in the society and the role of teachers to promote democratic values among the students. The Framework firmly believed that the teachers themselves should internalise the values of justice, liberty equality, secularism and then only can they interpret the same effectively to the learners. The Framework laid stress on 'Competency Based and Commitment Oriented Performance in Teacher Education' which has wider implications for social cohesion and harmony. The Framework thus identified ten competency areas as:

Conceptual competencies; curricular and content competencies; transactional competencies; competencies in other educational activities such as planning, organising morning assemblies; competencies related to teaching and learning materials; evaluation competencies; management competencies and competences related to community contact and co-operation. All these competencies are, first to be developed during pre-service teacher education stage and then updated and strengthened further recurrent in service teacher orientation and self directed professional development programmes.

The Curriculum Framework also identified 'five commitment areas' for teacher education. Which are: commitment to learner; commitment to society; commitment to profession; commitment to achieve excellence and commitment to basic human values.[13]

At the global level, realising the role of teacher very important in the present perspective, efforts are being made to increase the teacher effectiveness in teaching-learning process. On the world map, teacher is the focal point of all educational planning.

IIEP (International Institute of Educational Planning) and OECD (Organisation of Economic Co-operation and Development) have made several studies in fragile states and OECD member countries and have come to the conclusion that, teacher must be the priority in all educational planning because they are the heart of the teaching-learning process. Impact of teacher on pupil's learning is much greater as compared to other socio-economic variables.

Lorin W. Anderson (2004) in his article, 'Increasing Teacher Effectiveness' (IIEP Fundamentals of Educational Planning Series) emphasised the role of teachers as of crucial importance because teacher is the main human resource input to schooling that affects the learning outcomes.[14]

OECD admits, that issues concerning teachers are burning ones but these are not necessarily same in all regions and in all countries. IIEP studies show that teacher professional development has become a topical issue and teacher education has moved from training and one off workshops model to package and more to school based solutions.

Today, IIEP is very much involved in teacher policies in various OECD countries. In the context of present world, which is full of challenges, teacher's role is more vital and difficult as Director of IIEP Gudmund Herness (2004) recognised, ***"Teachers can't be left to cope on their own, they need updating, supervision and inspiration as well. This is particularly the case when a society is undergoing rapid change and old styles and models are constantly challenged – whether it is by phenomena such as economic change and mobility or technological changes providing the youngs with new behavioural models or advanced tools and gadgets.***[15] He further added that; ***"it is paradoxical that while the importance of education is increasing the role of the teacher is becoming more vital and difficult"***[16]

In the context of the aforestated competencies and commitments stressed by NCTE for teacher education programmes and teachers crucial role stressed by IIEP and OECD in the perspective of the overall challenges of the modern world including the peace threats, teacher beholds a central place in all educational process specially for peace.

Thus, a teacher has to realise that he is a mentor of his students, that there is a symbiotic connection between children and teacher, that he is blessed and truely in a position to mould the lives of so many children. Today, teaching is a huge responsibility and calling. Earlier it was believed that the parents should be the bed rocks of values but in the fast moving modern life both parents are working; families are nuclear; children start going to day care schools from their early age. Today children spend a large proportion of their time in schools. Hence in the present perspective, the responsibility of nurturing the child holistically, building his character and preparing him for a tough world rests equally with his teachers who are his mentors. The teachers have to instill some values in children such as honesty, integrity, a sense of self worth, responsibility, tolerance, compassion, respect for divergent opinion, humility and of course self discipline so that they can grow up to be peaceful and balanced human beings. If teachers have to teach values to children, they have to be role models, they have to practice what they preach, they have to lead children by examples.[17] On this account teachers need to be aware of the effects of their behaviour on students in and out of the class-rooms. Specially from peace perspective where education is to be delivered cautiously, a teacher must be able to critically evaluate his/her attitude, habitual mode of thinking and approach to teaching. In this respect, to develop the required knowledge, attitudes and skills among teachers from day care schools to the stage of higher education, a well thought and well organised system of Teacher Education is imperative today. Now it is high time when Teacher Education has to take major stake in the programme of Education for Peace.

Presently a great amount of time, energy and money is being spent on the Education for Peace at global and national level. At global level there are UNESCO, UNICEF and other international agencies as UN Department of Disarmament Affair (UNDDA) which are trying to promote the Education for Peace in various countries. UNDDA is implementing a project in the form of Peace and Disarmament Education in countries as Albania, Niger, Peru and Cambodia. Hague Appeal for Peace (HAP), The Centre for Research on Education for Peace (CERPE) at university of Haifa, Israel, The Earth and Peace Education Association International (EPE), New York are such other organisations at international level which are engaged in developing the new perspective of education for peace.

In India, various apex bodies of education, research and teacher's training and planning as NCERT (National Council of Educational Research and Training) New Delhi, NUEPA (National University of Educational Planning and Administration) New Delhi, NCTE (National Council of Teacher

Education) and various colleges of Teacher Education and N.G.Os as Gandhi Peace Foundation are exploring the frontier of, how to carry and implement the Education for Peace in the realm of Indian system of education. Teacher Education holds a major share in this system of Education for Peace.

Teacher Education for Peace: Is it possible

India has a large system of education confronting with problems of diversity regarding culture, language, religion and caste along with group conflicts in its social setup. Illiteracy, deprivation and poverty are another factors which hinder the promotion of peace in the Indian society.'

In the present context, building and promoting culture of peace through teacher education is really a great challenge not only for India rather for any other country through out the world.

Thus, if teacher education is to be organised for the transmission of peace in the present and future teachers and ultimately for the development of culture of peace in the educational institutions so as to make them conducive for the implementation of Education for Peace in the realm of class-room, the great questions confronting us are: What will be its structure and model? Will the teacher education demand planned and purposive approach?

NCERT after recognising the role of teachers very important and relevant in not only imparting knowledge but also in influencing the psychological emotional and spiritual growth of students (National Curriculum Frame Work, 2005)[18], has organised various orientation and training programmes for teacher educators on various issues and concerns related to the 'Education for Peace.' NCERT is aiming to help teacher educators understand their role as 'peace educators' and enable them to learn the ways and means of integrating peace in teaching learning process in and out of the class-rooms. The teacher educators are choosen for training and orientation to develop knowledge, skills and attitude in themselves first and further transact Education for Peace to trainee teachers in the colleges of teacher educations, at all levels. It is believed that such trained teachers will be carriers of peace and will be equipped with knowledge, skills and attitude, sufficient enough, to deliver peace oriented education in and out of class-rooms in schools.

The perplexing questions regarding Teacher Education for Peace in the present context of Indian society and the world scenario are:

- Are the teacher education programmes, developed in the perspective of high ideals and values, going to be sucessful?

- Are we not perceiving Teacher Education in isolation?

- Are the environments of present educational institutions and of surrounding societies not influencing teacher education complexes?

- Is the present atmosphere conducive for contextualisation and operationalisation of peace values in the teacher education programmes?

The unfortunate fact is that, the whole environment of the society and educational institutions are going down morally day by day. Today in the campuses of educational institutions; corruption bribery, rivalry, political confrontations, egoism, cynisism and nepotism have become omnipotent, In general, man is dehumanised due to ever increasing allurements of the material world, cut-throat competitions, declining state of social, emotional and civic security and erosion of moral and ethical values. In this situation, can we imagine that Teacher Education for Peace which is conceived in such a way that it has nothing to do with the global and societal tendencies prevalent in the world, is going to do miracle with the present (in service) and future teachers in changing their cognitive, conative and affective domain of personality. Hence, the programmes to achieve the ideals and higher aims of teacher education with reference to Education for Peace are going to remain futile and waste unless, thoughtful and deliberate efforts are made in the endeavor of educational process in the domain of Teacher Education.

Though, it seems to be dream to think about such ideal conditions which are pre-requisite and necessary to carry Teacher Education for Peace, even then creation of environment in and out of teacher education institutions conducive for the development and promotion of culture of peace is an inevitable reality which has to be realised at any cost, if we really and honestly want to implement teacher education programmes in the new perspective of Education for Peace.

If Teacher Education programmes are expected to prepare teachers, who will further develop the culture of peace and will carry the Education for Peace in the reality of class-rooms, all teacher education programmes should be evolved through Culture of Peace. Hence Teacher Education should be perceived in a large context of the huge system of education particularly in India. Teacher Education has to be perceived in totality whichever country may be. Yet, a question arises, is there any model of Teacher Education for peace which may be tried out in the present perspective? The solution remains in an hypothetical model which seems to be the last option before us. It may be a dream model which may be collectively tried out with wisdom and vigour, if we are really interested in promoting Culture of Peace in educational institutions through Teacher Education;

if we are really interested in transforming the culture of war into the culture of peace in educational campuses where our children and youths are safe and are not tending towards violence, criminal activities depression and suicides; if we are really interested in providing our children a peaceful and harmonious life to live.

A Dream Model of Teacher Education for Peace[19] (in Indian context) : Is it possible to realise

A hypothetical model of Teacher Education for Peace implies a model of the transactional process of Education for Peace through Teacher Education The transactional process is upside down, hence the hypothetical model is also upside down just like a miraculous 'Ashvathha Tree' described in Mahabharata (an Indian scripture). This tree grows upside down, its roots are in the sky and the branches are hanging upside down, penetrating into the earth. Likewise, Teacher Education programme with reference to peace transaction should start from the higher institutions of education. It means the process should start from the various departments and faculties of education in the universities and other apex bodies of educational research, training, planning and administration as NCERT (National Council of Educational Research and Training) New Delhi, NUEPA (National University of Educational Planning and Administration) New Delhi and NCTE (National Council of Teacher Education) New Delhi and similar other institutions of higher learning and teacher education.

The process should further pass through teacher educators to teacher-trainees (with peace oriented teacher education curriculum and pedagogy) and ultimately to school children (with the curriculum of Education for Peace through suitable pedagogical techniques) in their reality of class-rooms. This is ultimate ground where peace oriented teachers will write the message of peace in the hearts and minds of children. This is hopefully the ground where a generation will be shaped for future society living in peace and harmony.

The only fact which has to be taken care of is that peace transactional process through Teacher Education for Peace has to be carried out in peace oriented environment. The transactional process embodies peace education curriculum and training of pedagogical techniques for the transaction of the Education for Peace at every stage of Teacher Education. At every stage of the process, the first step should be to induce the 'will' or desire for peace among teachers. They should be made aware, why peace is an essential condition for the sustenance of human lives on the earth, and how peace can be approached, so that they could be awakened and could be ready to assimilate ideals and values pertaining to peace and further they would be ready to impart such education and create an environment to deliver Education for Peace in and out of the class-room.

Stages for Imparting Teacher Education for Peace

The various stages of the Teacher Education for Peace may be as follows:

Stage:-1

Academic Staff Colleges vis-a-vis Heads and faculties of University Education Departments and Affiliated Colleges

Academic Staff Colleges (ACSs) should organise orientation and refresher courses preferably on peace education which could be made obligatory to lecturers, readers, professor and even heads of the departments and principals of the affiliated and constituent colleges, it may be associated with promotion and increments in pay of teachers. Without preparing heads of the institutions, no institutional climate could be created which would be conducive for peace oriented education. Thus it may be emphatically suggested that heads should voluntarily and willingly attend the orientations for a very urgent and noble cause.

University Faculty As a Role Model

University departmental heads and faculties should be made to realise that they are the role models or the ultimate creators of peace. Hence they should be prepared to perform their roles. The process may be divided into two steps;

(i) Learning to Be.
(ii) Learning to Do.

Learning to Be

- Liberating their own minds from narrow feelings, fear, biases, complexes, unethical desire etc.
- Controlling and regulating their own emotions in conflicting situations.
- Making congenial interpersonal relationships with their colleagues, students and other staff members.

Learning to Do

- Functioning in a democratic and secular way.
- Encouraging healthy competition and peaceful co-operation in the institution and in the classroom.
- Creating congenial atmosphere by resolving conflicts.
- Accepting the differences and respecting diversities in the institution and classroom as well.

All this requires the mastery over the course content and pedagogical aspect of peace education and skills to deliver education or subject matter with reference to peace.

Course Content for Orientation programmes may be:

- Conceptual framework of peace education, and education for peace.

- Theoretical and practical aspects of Yoga and meditation.
- Nature and needs of human society.
- Criticism of wars and violence which include;

Fatal consequences of war, violence, bloody struggles and terrorism.

Disarmament and expenditure of defence.

- Social Justice.
- Human rights and duties (with special reference to teacher and students.)
- Stress management.
- Emotional Competence.
- Some of the scriptures which have practical utility in making peace, like Bhagwad Gita and other literatures of spiritual and socio-political thinkers as, Mahatma Gandhi, Martin Luther King Jr, J. Krishnamurti and others.
- Research findings of peace-studies and peace work, reports of various 'Culture of Peace Programme's by UNESCO and othe national level programmes.
- Relevant films which convey message of non-violence and other essential values.

Pedagogy (Teaching-learning mode)

The review of literature and documents on Peace Education and most recently on Education for Peace show that a number of teaching methodologies are available that can be tried out to inculcate and promote peace in and out of the classrooms.

In Orientation Courses, along with lectures, those methodologies and approaches should also be chosen and taken into account which could suit to the mind set of senior faculty members of university departments and heads of the higher education institutions. These may involve introspection, brainstorming, sharing views, dialogues, co-operative learning, participatory approach, value clarification, conflict resolution, techniques of mediation and jurisprudential model, etc.

The resource persons should demonstrate the methods by involving all the participants so that they can be prepared to handle the situations of conflict, controversies and tensions in their real work fields. They should be made aware of other approaches as, software and hardware self-instructional approaches/Role-playing and Idiographic etc.

Resource Persons

Resource Persons should have the following qualities. They should,

- Speak clearly;
- Have appropriate knowledge and skills of participatory methods and approaches;
- Have lesson plans in advance;
- Be organised;
- Be sensitive to trainees needs;
- Be relevant;
- Have good personality;
- Be enthusiastic and energetic;
- Be adaptable;
- Be encouraging;
- Create a positive learning atmosphere;
- Be a good listener and build on what the trainees say;
- Work from heart;
- Steer the discussions to them;
- Show good principles and provide clear example of sustainability;

For practical purposes, Academic Staff Colleges can invite the spiritual masters, management gurus, Yoga experts, councellors, subject experts and the experts of the different pedagogical approaches.

It is to be noted that at the first stage of the transactional process, the Orientation and Refresher programmes should be organised not only for Department of Education and teacher educators rather for teachers and heads of all faculties and departments of various subjects or discipline so that the university and college teachers in general could be equipped with the knowledge, skills and attitudes to handle the curriculum prepared (see chapter-V stage specific approach) to deliver Education for Peace at higher education stage, on account of the role of higher education as builder and promoter of peace.

Specifically, in the context of Teacher Education: training, orientation and refresher programmes should converge on the faculties and departments of education in the universities and colleges.

Stage-2

Departmental faculty vis-a-vis Teacher Educators (M.Ed & MA Students)

Faculties, trained and oriented and equipped with skills and knowledge in peace education by Academic Staff Colleges should be motivated to impart Education for Peace. At M.Ed. and M.A. (Ed) level, either course content of Peace Education could be kept separate or it could be integrated or infused with other relevant papers as, Educational Philosophy, Educational Sociology, Educational Psychology, History and Problems of Education, Guidance and Counselling etc. In the departments of universities, other than regular courses, project work, M.Ed. dissertations and D.Phil research work can be undertaken on the peace related topics.

Peace Transactional Model for Teacher Education (Indian Context)

Peace Transactional Model

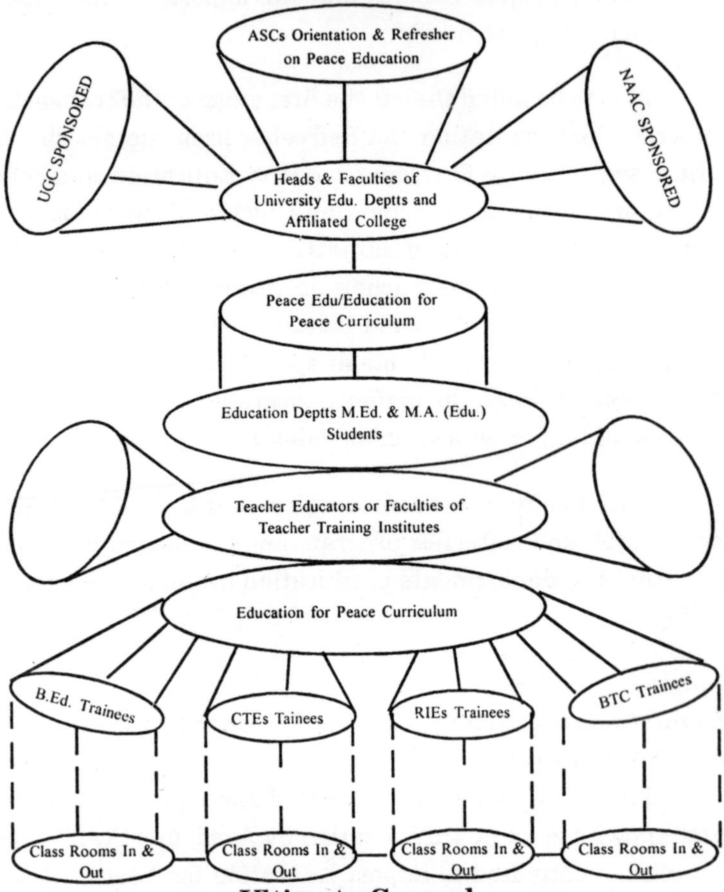

Ultimate Ground
(Secondary and Primary School Children)

ASCs : Academic Staff Colleges
UGC : University Grant Commission
NAAC : National Assessment & Accreditation Council
NCERT : National Council of Education Research & training.
NUEPA : National University of Educational Planning and Adminis tration

B.Ed. Courses, CTEs, RIEs, and BTC are the institutions of Teacher Education for the Secondary and Primary Schools.

Stage-3

Teacher Educators vis-a-vis Teacher Trainees

It may be hoped that, teacher educators imbued with peace related knowledge, understanding and skills are already transformed individuals but they further need orientation and refresher in Peace Education.

Teacher educators, or faculties of B.Ed. Colleges, Colleges of Teacher Education (CTES), Central Institute of Education (CIE) and Basic Training Institute should be properly oriented to deliver peace education as a separate subject along with pedagogic skills to deliver Education for Peace to their pupil teachers or teacher trainees. Training and orientation programmes should be exclusively organised by education departments of the universities, NCERT, NUEPA and other peace agencies.

In broader sense the course content and pedagogic skills may remain the same as that of the first stage throughout the transactional process, the only thing to be taken care of is - the target groups (teachers) to what category they belong and whom are they going to teach (secondary or primary level.).

Level of content and pedagogical skills should be according to the ultimate beneficiaries or children.

Stage –4

Trained Teachers (Pre-service and in-service) vis-a-vis School Children:

This is the ultimate ground of implementation of education for peace, where peace loving and peace oriented teachers can usher the children in an environment suitable for the Education for Peace. Through their positive attitude they can cultivate the culture of peace in their classrooms and schools.

This is hoped that the teachers trained in peace education could handle the curriculum designed for the Education for

Peace. At least they could be well aware of the fact that they are the agents of the transaction of peace process. In this respect they could know, what they have to be? And what they have to do? They are going to shape a generation for the future society, living in peace and harmony.

Out of optimism, it is hoped against hope that the hypothetical model of the Teacher Education for Peace may lead to its testing and experimentation not only in India but also in other countries having analogous structure of teacher education. The people may criticise and raise questions and even object to the proposed model offered here. Some of the obvious questions and doubts which may be raised are:

- The proposed model of Teacher Education is idealistic, this just can't work.
- At the Stage-I of the model of Teacher Education for the transaction of peace, how can Orientation and Refresher courses on Peace Education be made obligatory to heads of the education and teacher education institutions.
- How can university departmental heads and faculties be made to realise that they are the ultimate role models to lead the teacher educator in the process of Teacher Education for Peace.
- Is it possible to change the mind set of heads, managers and authorities in educational institutions only by making them to participate in the Orientation and Refresher courses on Peace Education. It can not be done on some body's demand because many individuals struggle throughout their life to change the mind set of other fellow members but do not succeed. The rapid change in a person's mental and affective spheres is not possible.

- In the periphery of Orientation and Refresher courses organised by Academic Staff Colleges and other institutions, teachers, experts and resources persons, all come from the society which has been already sunk into moral crisis. Thus, in the environment of egoism, mutual rivalry, jealousy, conflicts and cynicism, how can one expect that, all heads and authorities of education will meet together under the umbrella of 'Education for Peace' and will further extend the notion of Culture of Peace in their respective institutions.

- Earlier, education as a diversified means has been tried in various parts of the world but it has failed to help keep peace. There may be many more questions which may confront us while thinking about the testing and operation of the aforestated model of Teacher Education in the perspective of the Education for Peace. Some people may attribute this type of thinking impractical and Utopian, but what is the way out? Today each and every individual associated with educational enterprise and who is sensitive, understanding, thoughtful and really anxious about the future of our children and youths (who are presently living in violence and terror oriented world) is perplexed, how to organise 'Education for Peace' which is going to nurture the knowledge, skills attitudes and values pertaining to peace among the children and youths from day care schools to college and university education. Since conceptually 'Education for Peace' is a long term practice to nurture individuals for peaceful living. The nature of Education for Peace is holistic, hence it embraces the physical, emotional, intellectual and social development of children or individuals within the framework of human values. Thus, in the broader perspective the last solution seems to be, to take 'Education for Peace as a social mission and a joint endeavor of home, schools, colleges, universities, society, governments, policy makers, industrialists and ultimately the politicians.

In the present chaotic and turbulent world full of challenges, teachers should not be blamed and left alone on their own to perform their role in the premises of educational institutions rather they should be backed by home and society to carry their role, in the new perspective of education to establish Peace. Dr A.P.J. Abdul Kalam, our former President of India in 'Ignited Minds' writes: "A nation's wealth is the young generation of the country, when they grow up, who can be the role models? Mother, father and elementary school teachers play a very important part as role models. When child grows up, the role models will be national leaders of quality and integrity in every fields including politics, the sciences, technology and industry.[20]

Thus, presently teacher alone can not be a role model for his student rather any adult in home, family and in the society may be a role model for him. So in the new perspective, Teacher Education for Peace should be taken as a social mission and the combined endeavor of all agencies concerned with education. This is high time when Teacher Education programmes should combine knowledge, experiences and dreams pertaining to the building of peace on one hand, and joint effort of other people and agencies of education on the other in such a way so as to change the culture of war to culture of peace and non-violence in the world we live. This is the only way out, if the powerful force of education is to be fully and wisely used in mankinds' last chance to build a peaceful world.

References

1. Trever, Albert A (1939) *History of Ancient Civilization,* New York, Harcourt, Brace, p. 45.

2. *Ibid.*

3. Roger. D. Guimps, *'Pestalozzi: His Life and Work'.* translated by J. Russel, New York (1895).

4. Mitra, Veda (1964), *Education in Ancient India,* Delhi, Arya Book Depo, pp. 40-41.

5. Mohanty, J. (2003). 'Development of Teacher Education in India before Independence, *Teacher Education*, New Delhi, Deep and Deep Publication, p. 3.

6. Mookerjee, R.K. *Ancient Indian Education: Brahminical and Buddhist,* New Delhi, Motilal Banarsi Das.

7. Devi, R.S. *Origin and Development of Teacher Education in India,* S.N. Mookerjee (Ed), Vol. I, New Delhi, S.Chand and Company, p. 4.

8. *Ibid.*

9. http://en. wikipedia.org/wiki/Jiddu-Krishnamurti

10. Government of India (1966), Report of the Education Commission (1964-66). On Education and National Development, New Delhi, Ministry of Education, Government of India.

11. Government of India (1986), Report of National Policy on Education (1986), New Delhi Ministry of Human Resource Development, Govt. of India.

12. NCTE (1998), *Curriculum Framework for Quality Teacher Education*, New Delhi, NCTE.

13. NCTE (1998), *Competency Based and Commitment Oriented Teacher Education for Quality School Education,* New Delhi, NCTE.

14. Anderson, L.W. (2004), Increasing teacher effectiveness Extract from the preface of the book by T. Neville. IIEP, Fundamentals of Educational Planning Series. *News Letter* Vol. XXII, IIEP, Paris, UNESCO, p. 4.

15. Hernes, Gadmund (2004), Elevators and operators (editorial), *News Letter*, Vol. XXII, IIEP, Paris, UNESCO p. 2.

16. *Ibid.*

17. Birla, N. (2009) Leading by Examples; Times of India, Times Nation, Feb. 2.

18. NCERT (2005) *National Curriculum Framework (2005) A Position Paper on Education For peace*, New Delhi, NCERT.

19. Upadhyay, P. (2007). The Will for Peace: Induction and Transaction through Teacher Education, *Journal of Indian Education*, Vol. XXXII, Feb 2007, New Delhi, NCERT.

20. Kalam, APJ Abdul (2003), *Ignited Minds Unleashing the Power within India,* New Delhi, Penguin Books, pp. 36-38.

7

Education for Peace: Utopia or Reality

WHAT WOULD MAN BE without Utopia? He must aim at the Unattainable in order to realise the attainable and to make one step forward

-THOMAS MANN

Is Peace Possible?

Presently we are living in an insane world[1] which is in a state of confusion, conflict and in deep sorrow. We, the people, always strive to know and conceptualise theoretically the world where we can live in peace. We invariably theorise what the world should be and try to adjust ourselves to that idea as that world is possible where there would be no pains, miseries and sorrows. It is just like, that the people have not tried before to know and to eliminate the human miseries from the world and have not thought of making peace on this planet earth. In fact human miseries and pains have been always there in the history of mankind and people in the world have always strived to attain peace, inner as well as outer or global from time immemorial, but 'peace' as an 'end' has never been attained. Thus people have enough cause to believe that 'peace' is an Utopian notion; peace is just a dream island of perfect tranquility in an individual or in the world that can be ventured but cannot be captured. It is a common belief that peace in the world and peace in the inner self of human being is impossible to attain fully and permanently.

A peaceful state of mind of an individual, society and the world is the outcome of web of relationships among individuals, communities and the nations of the world, hence notion of peace is relational and associational. Peace can be realised if an individual lets another fellow individual to live in peace; a community lets another fellow community to live in peace; if a nation lets another neighbour nation to live in peace, that is why Mahavira said, "Live and let live". Peace cannot be achieved through demand, it is reciprocal; if you give it then you get it but in the present confused and brutal world, the principle of Mahavira seems to be failed. There are several evidences in the past human history and the history in making which show, how some people, communities and nations are indulged in fighting despite the various peace efforts from their neighbours. Jesus said, ***"Love thy Neighbour"*** how can you go on loving your neighbour when he is always ready to prick and fight. It is a psychological fact that some people, communities and countries enjoy violence, war, fighting and brute activities; they do not want to let other people other communities and other nations to live in peace; they do not believe in the principle of "Live and let live"; how can reciprocity be expected from them. If we take

As human beings we all want to be happy and free from- misery— we have learned that the key to happiness is inner peace. The greatest obstacles to inner peace are disturbing emotions such as anger, fear and suspicion, while love and compassion and a sense of universal responsibility are the sources of peace and happiness.

Unknown

peace in the international context, the current example of such tendency of the nations is none other than our neighboring country Pakistan. After the partition and independence of India, Pakistan vexed Kashmir and always remained a headache to it. Pakistan has been always indulged in disturbing the peace in India, sometimes by warring and rest of the time patronising and encouraging cross-boarder terrorism. The terrorist groups trained in training camps backed by Pakistan have created genocides and mass exodus of Kashmiri Hindus from Kashmir and continuous bomb blasts and massacres in various parts of India. The recent episode of terrorist invasion (26/11/2007) in Mumbai, India, was the heinous act conducted by a terrorist group backed by Lashkar-e-Taiba (a terrorist organization rooted in Pakistan). Despite various peace efforts by Indian Government, NGOs and peace talks between the leaders of both countries, no reciprocity from Pakistan is being received till now. The people of both countries suffer due to enemity and hostility caused by the leaders specially from Pakistan. Common people from both the sides undergo the sufferings caused by catastrophic effects of wars and terrorism.

There are several more examples in the world where disputes between the groups or between the nations are impossible to resolve and that cause a continued conflict among them and disturb the peace in the region. Such an example is the Palestinian Crisis which has drawn the attention of the whole world but seems to be impossible to resolve. The dispute between Israel and Palestine is deep rooted in the long history which shows a great paradox that the sacred heartland of Israel that claims to be the origin of world's three monotheistic religions —Judaism, Christianity and Islam, instead of being a place of

These religions, as lived and practiced by millions, hide behind their exterior piety a good deal of selfishness, social callousness and violence.

Swami Vivekananda-

peace and unity is a cauldron of hatred and terrorism. Since a long period in history the whole world is witnessing horrible wars between Jews and Palestinians. The name Palestine was commonly used to describe the whole area even by Jews until 1948 when Israel came into existence as a state. Both have faced cruel fate since centuries and have always found refuge and solace in one another. When Jews were illtreated by Romans and expelled from Spain, they were sheltered and protected by Arabs. The history of Israel/Palestine cannot be judged on regional standards because the land has been inhabited by different tribes, nations, ethnic groups and it has also withstood many wars and exodus of people from all sides; that is the reason it becomes so complicated when either group claims the right to assert that it is their land. The modern state of Israel has been acquired by Jews which they really fought for and deserved. The Jews have been disadvantaged in every possible manner and even massacred by Egyptians, the Romans, the English, the Russians, the Babylonians and most recently by Germans under Hitler's reign, hence the Jewish people want and deserve their home land. On the other side, Palestinians too have a history of persecution and many coastal towns were under the possession of their forefathers till recently a short time ago. Thus, Palestinians believe that what is now called Israel is nothing but part of their nation even if they get the West Bank and Gaza Strip. At the same time Jews believe that West Bank in Judia and Samaria is a part of their homeland even if Palestinian states were established there. The call for 'two states solution' or partition is not possible and cannot work. When we look from a distance at events in Israel and Palestine, it is natural to feel pity and helplessness because it is difficult rather impossible to judge, who should be held responsible for the tragedy we now see. Israel and the Palestinians both wish for peace but the manifestation is expressed by the horror of continuous wars. Various peace efforts have been made throughout the history, all failed, no permanent solution is found yet.

It is needless to go into past history. We have a long list of similar examples of conflicts, wars, invasions and terrorism throughout the globe presently. Few of them are, The US invasion in Iraq, Occurance of 9/11 terrorist attack on World Trade Centre, New York, and consequent "War on Terror" (i.e. bombarding and hostile attacks on Afghanistan) by the U.S. Israel's attacks on Palestine and Lebanon and so many such examples of military operations throughout the world which have diminished the lives of great number of people on this earth.

Along with Palestine, Israel and Lebanon, there are several fragile states (as they are termed) as Afghanistan, Angola, Kongo, Burundi, Kosovo Rwanda which have suffered prolonged conflicts and civil wars and are still facing challenges of wars and attacks. Mutual attacks, suicide bombings and kidnappings create fear and terror in the respective regions and impede the flourishing of working and personal relationships necessary for a human society. The ordinary daily life of people in these states habitually put human dignity to risk. Although fragile countries make up only 9% of the world population, they account for over half of the children out of school, a third of infants who die before the age of five and quarter of people living with HIV and AIDS. At the same time global warming, the escalation of food prices and internal and external shocks have an intensified impact on these fragile states. These states are far away from meeting Millennium Development Goal.[2]

History has shown us that our tendency to colonize and exploit other regions has always backfired. This planet can be made a happier, more peaceful place to live in. but the change will have to come from with in the hearts of all of us living here.

Chris Butler- Wisdom-

People of these countries try to emerge from crisis but fail due to fragility and continuous conflicts. There is no end of their distress and pain.

Thus at the international level, 'peace' seems to be impossible to hold and is a dream. A moral perspectives of the resolution of conflicts is meaningless unless all nations involved come forward to resolve the conflict by mediations of peace keeping bodies like UN and mutual dialogues but it never happens. Solutions of problems based on morality and ethics seem to be complicated and difficult to accept for the politicians and leaders of the suffering countries, they find 'war' the easy tool to combat the present problems. They don't believe in long term measures and they don't have patience to carry on those measures.

As far as peaceful existence of an individual in the present world is concerned, for him moral living is very difficult. Today the world is standing on the threshold of major psycho-social transformation and is fragmented into nationalities, religions, sects, Gods, races, castes, creeds, colour, gender and so on and so forth. All these fragmentations have pushed the world into confusing, conflicting and sorrowful state. Thus, most of the people find the old and conventional moral and ethical values inadequate and irrelevant in providing them inner strength to live in the present world. In the world, where a large population is living under poverty and severely difficult conditions, moral and ethical values do not find place in fullfilling their emotional and material needs. How can one expect that poor and hungry would live a moral life, can moral and ethical values remove physical ailments of man, his material poverty and distress? All though, there are some who want to lead a moral life but in the

History teaches that war begins when governments believe the price of aggression is cheap.

Ronald Reagan-

present chaotic, violent, confused and morally declining world, they find themselves entangled in moral conflicts and dilemma. The situation in the world is uneasy and disturbing for those who want to live peacefully by following moral and ethical values. The moral dilemmatic situation in the present world is a big threat to human civilisation.

Thus, the world today from individual to global level is in a big trouble. How can 'peace' be created is a perplexing question. History of mankind reveals that, "We have tried everything". In an effort to make the world a better place, thinkers from Greek philosopher Plato to German political philosopher and socialist Karl Marx have proposed numerous political ideologies. The results? An article in the journal 'New Statesman' said ***"We have not abolished poverty or constructed world peace. On the contrary, we seem to have achieved exactly the opposite. It is not as though we have not tried, we have tried everything from communism to the pure market, from the League of Nations to nuclear deterrence. We have fought too many 'wars to end wars' to believe that we know how to end war. The article continued, We began the [20th] century enthusiastically believing that the scientists would save us and we end it not believing a single word they say."*** In 2001 Emeritus professor of Economic and Social History at London University Eric Hobsbawn wrote that mankind's political systems ***"face an age when the impact of human action on nature and the globe has become a force of geological proportions."*** [3]

The solution or mitigation of these problems will require measures for which almost certainly no support will be found

The misery of men will continue to exist, until man's character changes.

Swami Vivekanand (The Complete Works of Swami Vivekanand,Vol. I)-

by country votes or measuring consumer preferences. This is not encouraging for the long term prospects of either democracy or the globe.

Seeing catastrophe staring mankind in the face, the world famous astrophysicist and best selling author Stephen Hawking asked; ***"In a world that is in chaos politically, socially and environmentally, how can the human race sustain another 100 years?"***[4]

Thus, the economists, scientists and philosophers looking at dismal peace records throughout the world show uncertainty about the human survival in the next future.

The past history of peace efforts for world peace is also a history of failures. Why is it so? It is a great reality that there are people, societies and countries in the world who are not interested in keeping peace, they are instinctively aggressive, restless and wicked, they are always engaged in creating terror and destruction, they are engaged in warfare and atrocities against civil societies. The human history is full of such examples where genocides and holocaust have been created by such people and individuals. The great monsters who have been responsible for massive crimes against humanity in the world history may be enlisted from Roman emperors to modern monarchs, military generals and political leaders as, Zar Necholas II (1894-1917 Russia,) Enver Pasha (1913-1918 Turkey), Stallin (1924-1953, USSR) Antonio de Salzar (1932-1968, Portugal), Hitler (1933-1948, Germany), Vladimir Lenin (1917-1924, USSR) Emperor Hirohito (1926-1989, Japan) Mao Tse-Tung (1945-1976, China), Mussolini (1922-1943, Italy), Ho-ChiMinn (1945-69, North Vietnam), Yahya Khan (1969-71, Pakistan). Pol Pot (1975-1979, Cambodia), Saddam Hussain (1969-2003, Iraq), Idi Amin (1971-1980, Uganda)[5] and so many political leaders of today. Presently a great monster is the global terrorism which has created a war like situation in the world and has shaken the whole human civil society. The armies of terrorists and militant groups as Talibans (supported by Al-Queda) are creating havoc and terror in human civil societies and have made the lives hell of affected communities, may be of Afghanistan or Pakistan Thus, in the world, demons always exist and destroy the peace of common innocent people. But it is not like that, humans have not got opportunities for peace. The great tragedy of human history is that, men have got several opportunities time to time to hold peace through religious, spiritual and political movements throughout the world but they lost them again and again. The reason was the lack of strong will and commitment among the aspirants of peace. After the two successive World Wars, creation of League of Nations, United Nations Organisation and its agencies (UNESCO, UNICEF etc.) were the attempts of the communities of the world to rebuild peace at the international level and further to eliminate the possibilities of wars and holocausts. from the world.

It is a great paradox that these international institutions were established to create legal and political alternatives for resolving international conflicts, preventing war, removing threats to peace but unfortunately the world seems to have achieved exactly the reverse. Thus, we have a past history which shows that the efforts were always being made by world community, opportunities were always being available to hold peace but good results were not necessarily the ultimate outcome.

Unconditional war can no longer lead to unconditional victory. It can no langer serve to settle disputes. It can no longer be of concern to great powers alone. For a nuclear disaster, spread by winds and waters and fear, could well engulf the great and the small, the rich and the poor, the committed and the uncommitted alike. Mankind must put an end to war or war will put an end to mankind.

John F. Kennedy

The Director General of UNESCO, Amadou-Mahtar M'Bow (1978) while addressing the special session of 'UN General Assembly on Disarmament' expressed his anxiety about increasing nuclear armament in the world and typifying peace, a balance of nuclear terror ***"We are offered, peace as one of a variety of possibilities which we have to seize hold of and defend, not as a necessity beyond our freedom of choice, we have to deserve peace and deserve it urgently..... today in the World, the balance of nuclear terror epitomizes all the dangers of our present hesitation between war and peace. It is in sense, the negative aspect of our wisdom. It is the fear of war, it is not yet confidence in peace".***[6] After more than three decades of UN General Assembly on Disarmament, no change in the face of world order is evident, rather the situation is opposite. Despite various disarmament treaties and agreements among the countries, all nations are involved in arms race either to secure their boundaries or to attack on neighbouring countries. Large scale smugglings and trading of most advanced nuclear weapons are evident on the world map. Presently Talibans have formed a huge army equipped with most advanced and sophisticated nuclear weapons and war accessories; they have depositories of weapons, either smuggled or snatched from the deputed American army in Afghanistan. Likewise in India, the terrorist groups-internal and cross border, also possess nuclear and sophisticated arms, kill innocent people and create devastations in civilian areas. Today, all over the world, terrorism is just creating havoc and horror before mankind by large scale destructions and massacres. Thus under the dreadful shadow of global terrorism and wars

We have had international crises upon crises, inflation, recession, unemployment and a growing concern about the country's ability to compete in foreign markets——People today are worried about the real possibility of nuclear war, the economy and the environment. *Researching the Readers*, The Milwaukee Journal (1984)-

on one hand and helplessness of UN and other apex international bodies on the other, fear and insecurity in people are unimaginable. How can peace be possible in this turbulent and brute world? Is there any effective means to create peace in the world without war seems to be a ridiculous question in the present perspective.

If we turn our focus from global to national level, the truth of the matter is that: if a country like India prepares for war or for combating terrorism, it has to strengthen its defence force and policing system which requires a great amount of financial and human resources. Consequently a great number of essential activities in the field of nutrition, health, literacy, education, techno-scientific development and safe-guarding of environment are curbed or even blocked solely for lack of attention and material resources. This in turn aggravates inequality and severe disparity in the society and brings about new situations of tensions not only at the societal level but also at the national level. This is a great danger to our security and sovereignty. Inequalities and lack of basic amenities in the society further create ground for the fertilisation of terrorism. In India itself most of the terrorist and militant groups in Bihar, Andhra Pradesh, Assam and other states are the outcome of unemployment among youths, poor condition of farmers, political and economic isolation of various communities in the states, some of the militant groups are the product of fanaticism created by more established religious fundamentalist organisations. Presently in India, a new breed of militants have been produced by separatist politicians on account of language and region only for the sake of vote bank politics.

Dream, Dream, Dream
Dreams transform into thoughts
And thoughts result in action.

Dr. A.P.J. Abdul Kalam (Ignited Minds)

In this alarming situation specially in India, to make the order in the society, what is involved here is both an ethical requirement and economic imperative. This implicates that, the social and political order should be based on ethics and fruits of economic development should necessarily reach all segments of the society. Is it possible today? Can our society and the present politics in the country be rejuvenated ethically? Can economic system based on pure markets be changed back to adopt Gandhian theory of economics based on social justice, which says, property should be deemed to be held in trust for benefits and welfare of all. A good and enlightened government itself could be a trust on the vast scale.[7] Is it possible in the regime of present governments constituted mostly by the criminals, history sheeters and self- centred politicians? The governments either at Centre or at the State have nothing to do with the benefits and welfare of all people rather than their own political gains. In the light of the present chaotic and disheartening scenario not only in India but all over the world, people have to think urgently and inevitably that, how can a world be conceived and created where relations of reciprocity would replace those of unequal exchanges, where difference in culture, colour, castes, religion and opinion would cease to keep alive injustice in all its forms and would instead begin a process of cross-fertilisation. They have to think again and again, how can they lay foundation for humanism which will embrace all the people of the world, in the absence of genuine peace.[8] Alas! Peace is a dream in the present world, it seems to be a pathless land. Is it possible to reform the present chaotic and turbulent world into a dream land of peace? **Thinking of such a world where peace would be the core of human lives seems to be nothing but Utopia.** Though this type of thinking is not

What ever you can do or dream you can , begin it. Baldness has genius, power and magic in it. Begin it now.

Goethe-

new, rather it has been pervading throughout human history from times immemorial. It is the matter of fact that peace loving people and communities of the world have always strived to seek peace, inner and global. Different measures and strategies have been adopted to establish peace, individual, societal and global. In search of a long-term means which could establish lasting peace in this world and could protect human race from the catastrophe of wars and terrorism, people have realised that, 'educating minds of individuals' could be the only strategy that can overtake the possibilities of civil wars and violence in this world.

Peace is Possible if......

In the present world of distress and sorrow, peace seems elusive and even impossible. Though there have been a lot of efforts by people to build peace in the world, lot of conferences, conventions, and talks at local, national and international level have been held so that leaders could talk about, how to attain peace. In fact every day we turn on the news of peace talks breaking down between two warring countries, factions and ethnic groups, but these efforts to attain peace fail because 'Peace' is not really talked about in the right perspective. People are looking for peace but in wrong places and therefore it cannot be found. As a matter of fact, peace should be looked upon inside oneself, not outside. One cannot ask other people or groups to attain peace, but when peace begins with oneself, then this can start a chain reaction which will eventually lead to world peace. Peace is an intrinsic quality that humans have. It is "an inner state of being of calmness, serenity and power.'

The important thing here is the awareness and knowledge that one can have that capacity and power to hold peace.

It isn't enough to talk about peace, one must believe it. And it isn't enough to believe in it, one must work for it.

Eleanor Roosevelt-

Knowing one's capacity for peace leads one to the path of peace. After one has been made aware of this ability the person or individual must practice discipline. Here discipline means controlling one's thoughts. Our thoughts influence our feelings, our feelings influence our habits, our habits influence our thoughts and so on.

A person must avoid negative thoughts, and must start positive thinking. By planting seeds of positivity, peace may be possible. If each of us as an individual begins to think more peacefully and positively on our own and act more peacefully at home, school, workplace and with others, then our community and countries will in turn become more peaceful places to live. Then if countries relate more peacefully, our world would become more peaceful. Thus, it is the individuals who make up the world, so it is up to each one of us to make the world peaceful.[9] This point of view relating individual peace to world peace is being held by various thinkers and spiritual leaders of today. J. Krishnamurti is the proponent of this idea. He explains as a matter of fact what the existing world is? Who is the creator of its problems, distress, miseries and sorrow? Where does its solution lie? and who is going to transform this world into a peaceful place to live?

J. Krishanmutri says, ***"The problems of the world are so colossal, so complex that to understand and so to resolve them, one should approach them in a very simple and direct manner. The solution is not to be found through***

Peace starts with in each one of us. When we have inner peace, we can be at peace with those around us. When our community is in a state of peace, it can share peace with neighboring communities, and so on. When we feel love and kindness towards other, it not only makes others feel loved and cared for, but it helps us also to develop inner happiness and peace.

14th Dalai Lama-

conferences, blueprints or through substitution of new leaders for old and so on. The solution obviously lies in the creator of the problem, in the creator of the mischief, of the hate and of enormous misunderstanding that exists between nations and human beings. The creator of the problems is the individual- 'You' and I not the world as we see it. The world is your relationship with another. The world is not something separate from you and me, the world is the relationship that we establish or seek to establish between each other. So you and I are the problem, and not the world because the world is the projection of ourselves and to understand the world we must understand ourselves. ***The world is not separate from us. We are the world and our problems are world's problems. So we are responsible for the frightful misery and confusion in the world and even impending war. To transform the world, we must begin with ourselves.***

Thus, the transformation of the world can be brought about by the transformation of oneself, because the self is the product and part of the total process of human existence.[10] But how can this transformation be brought about? How can one achieve peace? Krishnamurti further adds ***'Man cannot come to it through any organisation, through any creed, through any dogma, priest or ritual, not through any philosophical knowledge and any psychological technique. He has to find it through the mirror of relationships, through the understanding of the contents of his own mind, through observation and not through intellectual analysis or introspective dissections."*** [11]

To transform oneself, self knowledge is essential, without knowing who you are, there is no basis for right thought and without knowing yourself there cannot be transformation ...... To know yourself, there must be awareness, the alertness of mind in which there is freedom from all beliefs, from all idealisation because beliefs and ideals give you a colour, perverting true perception ..... The knowledge of oneself demands honesty and clarity of thought. The understanding of what you are, whatever it be – ugly or beautiful, wicked or mischievous – the understanding of who you are without distortion is the beginning of virtue.[12] It is thus, the beginning of one's transformation. Only such virtuous persons or individuals may help the society and ultimately the world to transform.

Knowing oneself needs training and discipline of one's mind. Self knowledge cannot be given by another person, it is not found through any book. We have to discover ourselves and to discover oneself only needs – the intention to find out, to search and to inquire deeply one's real self, i.e. what he is and further to get freedom from what he is. The process of understanding ourselves is not an isolating process, withdrawal from the world, because one can not live in isolation.

To be is to be related and there is no such thing a man relates in isolation. It is the lack of right relationship that brings about conflicts, misery and strife; however small our world may be, if we can transform our relationship in that narrow world, it will be like a wave extending outwards all the time. Gradually we learn to discover and observe the activities of human beings right throughout the world; why they have become what they are, after forty thousand years of evolution; why they are killing each other; destroying each other; exploiting each other; why man has divided the world into nationalities, religions, Jews, the Arabs the Hindu, the Muslim and so on. Moreover we learn to look together why man has become, what he is, cruel,

If the world is to move away form the brink of terror, then new approaches, new combinations should play a vital role in the evolution of such an imaginative sprit.

Harvard Education Review, 1984 Aug.-

destructive, violent, idealistic and in the world of technology where men are doing astonishing things of which most of us are unaware; why after thousands of years of wars, shedding tears, a human being through a long period of time, is actually behaving in this manner........Man has divided the world- where there is division, there must be conflict. This is a natural law, which is what is actually taking place in the world. Why has man become what he is inspite of great experience, inspite of great knowledge, inspite of vast technological advancement: why has he remained more or less what he has been for 40,000 years; why? Is it because our mind, our brain is programmed to be a Bengali, to be a Muslim, to be a Hindu and so on? Is our brain prorammed, thinking in a conventional, narrow limited way? Why are human beings being programmed as Christians, Muslims and Hindus, believing in certain doctrines, certain beliefs and certain principles; perhaps for the last thousand years. Thus, our brains are conditioned to be this or that, to behave in a certain manner, to enjoy, to suffer, to have a great burden of fear, uncertainty, confusion and the ultimate fear of death. Does one ever realise how our brain is acting, thinking, looking? Our brain is conditioned to that particular thinking and there is a whole group of people, professors, scholars, writers, including the communists with their guru Marx who says that the human brain will always be conditioned; it can never be free; you can modify; that conditioning by environmental influence; it can always be modified, changed here and there; but actually the human brain can never be free. Where there is limitation there must be conflict.

In nutshell, according to J. Krishnamurti, it is the individual who is responsible for all the problems in the world. He is the creator of all confusions, miseries, panics and sorrows in the present world. So to transform the world into a better place to live, the process should start from the individuals. To transform oneself, an individual should have an honest intention to know himself, he should have capacity to search and inquire deeply into his real self that is, what he is. He should be able to realise, how his brain is acting, thinking and looking at others, or the outside world. He should be aware of how his mind is conditioned to his particular conventional beliefs and thoughts so that he could get his mind free from such condition. If total freedom is not possible, at least he can modify such conditioning through learning experiences. Thus 'peace' in the world is possible if and only if each individual is transformed into a peaceful human being. This requires conscientious training and discipline of minds of the individuals. Likewise, Gandhian concept of peace also emerges from individuals and extends to broader global levels. Gandhi's prescription for peace is nothing but the transformation of individuals into truthful and non-violent human beings through the training of Satyagraha. The technique of Satyagraha had been already applied to organise and train people and communities to oppose the oppressors during the freedom struggle in India. Today, at global level, the world community is again confident and hopeful that 'Peace is Possible'. The people are positive to 'peace' as much expert research has been done indicating that 'Peace is Achievable.'

The experts (The Seville's statement on violence, 1986) have shown rigorous scientific evidences and refute the myths, that human beings are pre-disposed to violence; that we have inherited a tendency to make war from our animal ancestors; that war or any other violent behaviour is genetically programmed into our nature; that in the course of human evolution, there has been a selection for aggressive behaviour more than for other kinds of behaviour; that humans have a violent brain. How we act is shaped by how we have been conditioned and socialised; that war is caused by instinct or any single motivation.[14]

UNESCO'S Culture of Peace Program and the extensive research of the large volumes of resource materials reveal the positive message to the world and show how peace is achievable. Stewart (Director Canadian Centres for Teaching Peace) have prescribed **'The Peace Formula'.**[15]

To achieve peace, the following variables must be in place as:

- ***A Credible government(s) code of ethics***

In simple terms of the things they think, say or do, government (s) must be able to be relied upon, to be truthful, fair, build good will and better relationships and strive for the benefit of all concerned.

- ***An international system of justice***

It is not hard to imagine that an international system of justice is necessary for crime against humanity, world environment and other international matter. At the same time, there must be reliable and proactive Conflict and Dispute Resolution Systems for parties who are willing to voluntarily work together to a solution, to avoid the necessity of going to court and most importantly to avoid conflict.

- ***A global sustainable economy***

There must be proper economy to provide reasonable employment and eradicate poverty and hunger. Nobel Prize winner Amaratya Sen has shown us how systematic public action can eradicate the terrible and resilient problems of starvation and hunger in the world in which we live. However economy must also be in balance with this small planet's ecology. This is probably the most difficult challenge. The Union of Concerned Scientists (amongst others) has issued a warning to all of humanity to change habits lest our planet Earth be irreversibly mutilated. ***"A great change in our stewardship of the earth***

and the life on it, is required, if vast human misery is to be avoided and our global home on this planet is not to be irretrievably be mutilated." It will take only co-ordinated action at the world level, in this respect no individual nation can remain disconnected from the rest of the world.

- ***A universal access to competent education system***

This principle is basic and simple and is included in the Universal Declaration of Human Rights for good reasons. Particularly, the education of women is key to both economic and peace development." The full participation and empowerment of women is essential to the development of a culture of peace —— Women's skills of exchange, co-operation and solidarity, as well as their experience of giving birth, bringing up the next generation and managing informal economies, are all essential to the evolution of a culture of peace... Women in all societies are the transmitters of the history, customs and traditions of their people. They are the key to the development of a culture of peace, which cannot be superimposed upon society, but must evolve from it. "Today, the very basis of the educational system must change. Everyone must be educated for peace. As Albert Einstein said, ***"Peace cannot be kept by force, it can only be achieved by understanding."***

- ***A compassionate health and welfare system***

This principle is also included in the Universal Declaration of Human Rights. Within a framework of Universal Human Rights and Responsibilities, the more privileged have a humanitarian responsibility to help the under privileged.

Every nation's level of internal (and often external) peacefulness is a result of the strength of these factors mentioned in Peace Formula. By extension, the world's level of peacefulness is a result of the strength of these factors. By strengthening these factors and the world may become more peaceful. Peace and the Formula for Peace, is measurable and manageable. After prescribing Peace Formula, Stewart further adds, what we have, therefore is a management or leadership challenge. Now, the formula to achieve peace is known and we currently have the knowledge, technology and infrastructure to achieve peace so what is the problem? The problem is Motivation. World leaders have not been motivated to work together in co-operation to achieve worldpeace. And the world's populace have not been motivated to motivate their political leaders.

We have a global problem that will require a global solution. This will take leadership at a global level that we all will follow. The United Nations is well placed to provide this leadership. However the United Nations would have to be reformed to undertake this honorous responsibility.[16]

Presently world has witnessed the helplessness of UN so in a recent article in 'Foreign Affairs' entitled, "Saving the UN", U.S. Senator Jesse Helms writes, The United Nations was originally created to help nation-state facilitate the peaceful resolution of international dispute. However, the United Nations has moved from facilitating diplomacy among nation-state to supplanting them altogether. Boutros Ghali in his 'Agenda for Peace' declared.... "The time of absolute and exclusive sovereignty...... has passed. Its theory has never matched reality"....... Such thinking is-in step with the nearly global movement towards greater centralization of political power ..... This process must be stopped.... UN reform is much more than saving money ... There must be termination of unnecessary committees and conferences... In addition to wasteful conferences like Beijing Women's Summit ... the United Nations continually sponsors workshops, expert consultations, technical consultations and panel discussions... most of these can be terminated at a savings of millions of dollars... The time has come for the United Nations to be reformed quickly and dramatically"[17]

The reform of United Nations is must, for if the UN dies then the globe and everyone on it will be at tremendous risk. Only the rich and powerful may prosper, and most certainly, the masses of poor and even middle class may perish at higher rates. Although the globe is not at the brink yet, warnings are that we may be there within fifty years more or less, and it is timely for our world leaders to make choice now.

Apart from the approach to the problem of leadership from the top down, a process should be at the same time from bottom up.

Today, more than ever before, civil society is experiencing a proliferation of non-governmental organizations (NGOs) in which individuals can engage in non-violent action for peace and justice. Moreover, with the emerging world communication network, they are increasingly able to link their struggle on a global scale. These are perhaps the most important development in the movement for a culture of peace, because the transition must take place in the minds of individual men and women through the process of action and growth.

Increasingly the energy and scope of NGOs is linked directly to the UN, both as a source of ideas and inspirations and as powerful multiplier for the universal principles of the organisation. It is also upto young people to take up the task of building and cultivating a culture of peace in the next generation. Citizens if supported by international networking, can play a key role in peace-building.

Finally, citizens must have a faith that peace is not only desirable but possible. Stewart further adds; Each of us must decide if we are part of the problem or part of the solution. ***The world is dangerous not because of those who do harm, but because of those who look at it without doing anything.*** Stewart further prescribes National Culture of Peace Programme as recommended by UNESCO's Culture of Peace Programme.[19] The essence of a Culture of Peace Programme is to address the roots of the problem as a common cause, to the benefit of everyone without diminishing any other. Education is the principal means to build a culture of peace.

A National Culture of Peace Programme would raise the profile mobilizing resources, organisations and public opinion. It will include actions to support participatory communications, networking and free flow and sharing of information and knowledge. Education is a principal means to build a culture of Peace, and hence, action would be taken to develop education, training and research for peace and non-violence. Ultimately, informed voters can provide direction to our leaders, motivating them to take necessary action to build peace in our communities and world.

Hence, if the majority of the world adheres to UNESCO'S Culture of Peace Programme, the world will be a much better place and mankind will evolve to a much higher level.

Finally, suitably tailored Formula for Peace as mentioned above, applies equally to building peace at the individual, family, community, national and world levels. Now, it is urgent to implement this formula It is particularly upto those of us individuals, communities and nations that are relatively prosperous to take responsibility for change - the poor and distressed are not able.[20]

Moreover, in the world there is a search for new leadership. With a new hope and confidence, people are attempting the task of building peace. They believed that a breakthrough in leadership is required which can turn the movement around the world.

President Obama is presently introducing a massive programme to encourage volunteerism amongst the youth in United States but it is the call of today that such programme of volunteerism should extend to the globe. The Alliance for the New Humanity (ANH) under the Presidentship of Deepak Chopra and Sahabhagi (an initiative of the Times Foundation) in India are attempting collectively to create the leadership of the future by focusing on social transformation through breakthrough training programmes and visionary leadership. ANH and Sahabhagi are attempting to begin a programme to teach leadership skills, based on spiritual values in schools in India. They are involved in such a grass roots volunteer programme which is supposed to hold promise of creating a breakthrough in leadership skills and would create a new humanity. The young students are offered to join this volunteer programme as a part of their education.[21]

In the light of the Prescriptions, efforts and various programmes by individuals, NGOs and international agencies like UNESCO (UNESCO'S Culture of Peace Programme) mentioned above, a new hope for peace is being created. Since efforts are going to be linked through communication networking, it may be hoped that one day all individuals, communities and NGOs under the global leadership will put their best to achieve peace in this world, this is a hope out of hope at last.

But alas! in the present chaotic and the fragmented world, this new hope again staggers under the ifs and buts. The possibility of peace is conditional. Peace at the individual, national and global level is possible if and only if the prescribed formula and principles are applied sucessfully in the reality of the world. The basic principle hidden in all formulae and prescriptions is, **'to change the minds of individuals by education'.** The transformation of individual is essential to transform the world and this can happen only by training and discipline of the minds of individuals.

Educating minds of people: Is it possible

Now on the basis of expert researches on peace, there has been sufficient rationale to think that 'educating minds of individuals' is an ultimate approach to lasting peace in the world. This is why UNESCO found necessary to attack the roots of the problems related to wars and international conflicts by means of action to influence the minds of men by developing international understanding through education and making the most effective use of the mass-media. The UNESCO called this programme a 'Moral Disarmament'. The UNESCO believed that, educating minds could only produce results itself as far reaching changes. The UNESCO has recognised 'the communication' between peoples and nations, the foundation of peace and assume particularly that the regular dissemination of free and responsible information drawing on findings of extensive studies in psychology, sociology, economics and history will throw light on human behaviour and will sweep away cultural prejudices, social and economic inequalities and will bring men closer to each other.[22]

From its very inception, it is believed that UNESCO is playing the role of peace builder by developing and supporting the educational, scientific and cultural programmes throughout the world. The recent Culture of Peace Programme by UNESCO is significant effort to develop culture of peace through education. Undoubtedly UNESCO is doing its job with devotion, competence and all the effectiveness its resources permit. But it cannot impose its will, the UNESCO can only persuade and convince and appeal to reason and common sense of people.

Inspite of the genuine intensions and efforts of UNESCO, UNICEF along with different national and international agencies, organisations, people's movements, governments' policies of education, conference and conventions, no significant change in attitude and actions of people and the nations have been found. Instead, world wide human society is sunk in the whirl-pool of wars, terrorism and moral dilemma. It appears that all efforts are insufficient, rather ineffective to influence the minds of men. What is the reason? Are they not striking the will of people to live in peace and harmony? Are they not able to gear up the motivation and aspiration of the people to make the world a better place to live? The questions are very difficult to answer but very basic and urgent.

Today humans are awaked and are trying to know the root cause of turmoil in the world, they are ready to combat the threats for the sake of future sustenance of human lives. This seems to be an awakening period in the history of mankind. Now we have arrived at the threshold of a new era where we can think that, war and bloodsheds can be averted because of the infinite potential of human spirit, will and aspirations. If wicked people can unite and constitute huge army to fight, to create terror and to make mass destructions in the world so why not peace loving people may combine to build peace on this planet earth. The only possible way out is to induce "the will" or desire for peace among people. This is the high time when the people of the world still have to want peace badly enough and with sufficient imagination and courage for it to come to pass.

Today it is a good sign that mankind has at last become aware of its existence and is ready to reconcile at societal, national and global level. The recent example is an alarming

There is nothing so likely to produce peace as to be well prepared to meet the enemy.

George Washington-

and rock hurling event of terrorism, 26/11(2007) in Mumbai, India and consequent reactions of people not only in India but also of the people of United States, Israel and of the whole world. Today, people are ready to combine to fight against terrorism. Never before in the history, the world community was so concerned and charged to attack the roots of the problem, though most of the people and nations are in favour of aggressive and hostile forces to combat the problem. After terrorists act (9/11/2001) on World Trade Centre New York, former President of America, Mr. George Bush declared "War on Terrorism" and sent the American Army to attack on Afghanistan. After so much bombardment and blood-shed America gained nothing, Today, the approach of the present Pesident Barack Obama is different. According to him, the notion of "War on Terrorism" is nothing but the counter terrorism which further aggravate the intensity of terrorism caused by the hostile groups. So we have to take 'global terrorism' as a challenge and must combat to finish it as early as possible (but by intelligent means).

As mentioned before, efforts are being enforced from UNESCO to community level (from top-down) as well as from community level to UNESCO (from bottom-up). Governmental and more specifically Non-Governmental Organisations are trying their best to make people alert and aware to combat terrorism. Most of the NGOs are attempting to educate people for volunteerism; efforts are interlinked through communication network. It can be said that the people of the world community are ready to reconcile and combined to attack the root cause of the global violence. Now, the nations have understood that they cannot exist in isolation; rather their problems are interconnected and ultimately disturb the peace of the world.

The present global situation is compelling the nations to think globally and act locally and this is the best formula for

Even peace may be purchased at too high price.

Franklin-

peace not only at the national level rather at the global level. Thus, in Indian perspective, people must think to save our country and its sovereignty but with reference to global peace. We, the people of India, are awakened today to combat the present anarchic and violent situation caused by external as well as internal forces, we cannot sit idle and depend on the actions of our super- power friends. So we must think 'how to begin the process'. It is the crucial time to first clean our own house. India needs a total constructive change in its political system. (which is the greatest malady of Indian life). The present political scenario is the root cause of all problems and miseries in Indian life so we have to think how can we clean our democratic system? How can we end the lawlessness and anarchy which are already the order of the Indian society? Today people of India are desperate to resolve the problem and to create a good government at last. It is a good sign, they should be motivated to hold their drive firmly. This is a ripe time for good people to arise, awake and combine to fight the evil forces pervading the whole Indian society. The drive should extend to the world in larger context. Volunteer Programmes are already running in patches throughout the world, the only requirement is to link them in broader context of global peace. The problems of terrorism (by external forces) and prospective wars cannot be solved without mediation of world leadership (i.e. UN which is loosing its credibility and there is hue and cry to reform it in near future.) Anyway, mankind should go on aspiring for peace at the individual, societal, national and global level. They must not surrender before the evil and negative forces pervading in violent and materialistic world, if it is done so, the survival of human society would be at stake. Today, it is not the time to see and review the track records of mankind's failure to build

One day we must come to see that peace is not merely a distant goal we seek, but that it is a means, but which we arrive at the goal. We must pursue peaceful ends through peaceful means.

Martin Luther King, J.r.-

peace in the world, rather it is the ripe time to step forward and translate the dream of a peaceful world into reality. This only needs an army of courageous, brave and good people who can stand firm and move forward against ferocious streams of evil forces. If huge armies of terrorists organizations and militant groups can be constituted out of fanaticism in the name of Jehad, why not armies of noble men may be constituted in the name of one religion, that is 'Peace. To combat the threats to human lives today there is need of army of such courageous and vigorous people who would end war and terrorism by non-violent and intelligent means. We have fought too many wars to end war, now we have last chance to combat war and terrorism by awakening the human soul and by operationalising the ideas and intelligence of human minds. Albert Einstein had said in 1934; ***"We stand therefore, at the parting of the ways, whether we find the way of peace or continue along the road of brute force, so unworthy of our civilization, depends on ourselves.***[23] This conflicting situation is still existing, when we have to choose the path. Hence, at the crossroad of human civilization, we have no option other than to choose the path of peace for the sustenance of human lives on this earth. In fact, in the present world, to think about the other way round, that is the path of peace is not beyond reality. This is the great truth that, in the present world there is a large population of people, much larger than the population of war loving, aggressive, murderous and wicked who are peace loving by nature and has courage and power to struggle against the currents of violent, destructive and negative forces present in the world. Their actions are commendable. How can we forget the past history where we tasted the fruits of the endeavors of such people. Specially, we, the people of India, can never forget the

Imagine all the people living life in peace. You may say I'm a dreamer, but I'm not the only one. I hope someday you'll join us, and the world will live as one.

Johan Lennon

contribution of Mahatma Gandhi who concretised and operationalised the principles of truth and non-violence in the form of 'Satyagraha'. He organised and trained people to follow Satyagraha and non-violent means to combat the political oppressors (Britishers) He by his magical personality and leadership contributed largely in the attainment of freedom of India. Gandhi has shown the world, how non-violent means can be used to achieve the great goals. Similarly world history reveals how quakers in England in Seventeenth century resisted Cromwell's forced conscription in British country side. Today so many Quakers are still doing commendable work in the developing and the developed countries alike. They don't believe in physical fighting but rather non-violent struggle for peace and justice. The oldest organisation of Quakers is the 'American Friends Service Committee, (Philadelphia) which still carries on its programme as an expression of belief in a faith in the power of love and non-violence to bring about change. The Committee has several regional centres in the United State.[24] Not only in America but throughout the world such organisations and committees of people are engaged in resisting the wars, violence and oppressions by non-violent means, only the style of functioning varies in the different parts of the world. The religious and pacifist movements not only in India but through out the world are unlimited. **Unfortunately these movements of people are not glorified as that of wars in the history of mankind**. Today, spurred by an awareness of the terror of nuclear weapons and political oppressions, educators through out the world are questioning the traditional notion of security that comes from being armed and are creating a new type of education that empowers people by asking them, What kind of society they want to inhabit? They are just stimulating people to use their skills and professional status to help create the new social order that promotes a world based on peace and justice.[25] Now we are at the threshold of human history where we cannot afford to be indifferent to the actions of such people, rather it is an obligation and responsibility of ours to join them and reinforce their actions to promote peace on this earth. In this connection, a quotation of an Irish Statesman, Edmund Burke seems to be relevant that, ***"All that is necessary for the forces of evil to win in the world is for enough good men to do nothing.***[26] So in this perspective, people and societies should be first awakened to realise the importance and urgency of peace in the present violence ridden and morally declined human world and next they should be stimulated to move forward to seek the ways and means to eliminate the catastrophe of war, fear of terrorism, injustice, oppressions of all kinds and moral dilemma in the human society and finally they should be encouraged to participate in activities bringing peace and harmony in this world.

Now people must realise that peace is the pre-condition of human survival and sustenance of human society. So there is no option other than to build peace at the individual and global level at any cost.

All religions, philosophies, scriptures, the sages, the saints and seers have indicated paths to peaceful co-existence of human beings and human societies. Buddha, Mahavira, Guru Nanak, Jesus Christ, Sufi Saints, hermits and many other enlightened souls in the world have shown us the paths of moral and spiritual living to attain peace. Now we have choice, either to follow the prescribed paths to peace which relate individuals to the larger world or to surrender before brute forces.

The past history of failures does not implicate that we should not strive further to build and promote peace in the world. Anyway the need and urgency of peace is inevitable, it is the first and the last aspiration of mankind. So if we really desire for the peaceful and harmonious state of the world, we do not have option other than to start again and again to pursue the endeavor.

The path of peace is very rough and difficult to follow in the midst of restless,, agitated and violent world. This only needs a strong will or desire among people to march forward. In the present state of the world only a strong desire or the strong will for peace would be motivating and stimulating force to carry on and reinforce the movements or steps of people towards peace.

At the present juncture of human history, it is imperative to ask, how can infinite potential of human spirit be explored? How can 'will' and 'drive' to attain peace be induced in people? The answer lies in educating the minds of people. With reference to the ideas of J. Krishnamurti, Mahatma Gandhi and others 'educating minds' solely implies the training and discipline of individual's mind and in this reference 'educating mind' is exclusively an individual endeavor to reform oneself. The transformation of the world begins with transformation of the individuals. But in the context of the present world where education refers to 'mass-education' or educational system of any nation, 'educating minds' imply educating minds of people in general so as to establish peace, harmony and universal brotherhood at the individuals, societal and the world level. In this reference, it is needless to further repeat, how 'Education for Peace' has been considered the best strategy to influence the minds of men and sow the seeds of peace in the human soul. Hence, in this respect, to transform the world, the only attempt may be to reorganise and rejuvenate the whole existing conventional educational system so as to develop the culture of peace throughout the world.

Education for Peace: Is it Utopia

Since in the present insane world, full of confusion, conflicts and sorrow, 'Peace' seems to be impossible to attain at the individual and global level as well, therefore a great perplexing question still remains, whether 'Education for Peace' is also a Utopia or is it possible to realise Peace in this world? This suspicion further emanates argument whether Education for Peace is an ideal approach to peace or is it merely an instrument to achieve an ideal or ultimate goal of human life (i.e. peace) which seems to be an unattainable dream?

Since 'Peace' is the tranquil state of mind and soul of an individual, a harmonious state of society and bond of universal love and brotherhood in the world, hence it is always susceptible to eruptions of disturbances. Peace is a momentary and transitory state of the mind of an individual, a temporary pacification in the society and the world. Thus, peace is not permanent and cannot be; it is very sensitive to hold; its endurance is possible only by following and retaining certain moral values and social ethics and virtues of life by the individuals, societies and nations by and large. In this respect, Education for Peace is expected to aim at :

- making people aware of their existence and threats to their survival;
- inducing the 'will' or desire for peace among the individuals;
- inculcating the set of values among the individuals so that they can live peacefully with others.

The conceived notion of Education for Peace again emanates a question, are we not expecting much higher ideals from Education for Peace as it is going to function in isolation? We must remember the fact that education is a social process

Nonviolence which is the quality of the heart, can not come by an appeal to brain.

Mahatma Gandhi –

and is carried out in the framework of a society, a nation and ultimately the world, hence it is naturally vulnerable to the influence of vices and virtues pervading in the surrounding society. The education, thus planned and organised in the perspective of peace is going to be enveloped by such environment where violence, terror, exploitations, oppressions and corruptness have become the order of day to day life. The people who are associated with such type of education and the people who are responsible to implement and carry out such education as ministers, policy makers, bureaucrats, heads of the educational institutions (from day care schools to the universities), teachers, other functionaries and ultimately the parents and families, all come from every nook and corner of such surrounding societies. Thus education, inevitably, is highly influenced and pressed by the complex and negative forces present in the surroundings.

As far as India is concerned, education has been always for 'Peace' but gradually education became ineffective in influencing the Indian society. As a result the society continued to decline morally and all types of agitations, confusions and restlessness entrapped the Indian life.

After independence of India, to see the ineffectiveness of education, various commissions and committees showed their concern and anxieties. Invariably all Education Commissions and Education Policies pointed out the declining state of the Indian society amidst the techno-scientific development of the nation. They have continuously shown their worries about the prevalent education system which has limited scope to educate the minds of children and youth by inculcating moral, spiritual and ethical values. The commissions time to time suggested various measures to orient education towards the inculcation of values, but the thoughtful endeavors of various commissions and policies in India got impetus when at the eve of 21st century, the General Assembly of the United Nations proclaimed the year 2000 as International Year for the Culture of Peace and decade 2001-2010 as the International Decade for a Culture of Peace and Non-violence for the Children of World.[27] According to Declaration and Programme of Action for the Culture of Peace adopted by the UN General Assembly (1999) and UNESCO's Culture of Peace Programme not only education but NGOs and other civil society organisations were also urged to contribute to the global movement for the development of peace. Since then, after the call of UN General Assembly, apex institutions of education and research in India are engaged in following the pursuit. The team of educators and responsible persons associated with educational enterprise are vigorously and seriously involved in planning and developing the objectives, curriculum, teaching methodologies and teacher education programme for the new perspective of education for peace. A huge amount of time, energy money and human resource is being spent in the name of the development of education in the framework of 'Culture of Peace'. Higher education institutions and the universities are just organising conferences, seminars and workshops on stereotyped subjects as human rights, women related issues and environmental concerns. After the 26/11 episode of terrorists invasion in Mumbai, various intellectual and public forums have shown their fear and anxiety regarding security of human life and are engaged in discussing the root cause of the present threats to the lives of people, and its implications in the near future. The matter of fact is that, mostly conferences, seminars and symposia are drowned in general theoretical deliberations and discussions without practical implications with serious notes.

Unhealthy societies threaten individual survival, that something can be done to change the nature of social reality and that education provide the means to build a better society.

George Counts (Dare the Schools Build New Social Order)-

It has been increasingly clear till now, that the notion of 'Education for Peace' has been merely a matter of intellectual exercise and academic endeavor limited to academia. Thus, a question confronting us is, if we are really concerned with translating Education for Peace into reality, who is going to implement and operationalise such education? Now, we have to look into the ground realities within which Education for Peace is to be materialised. Since implementation and operationalisation of education in any country is a collective effort of the people from all segments of the society as government(s), politicians, bureaucrats, managers and heads of the institution (schools, colleges and universities), teachers and parents. If education aims to develop a culture of peace, all have to contribute to this endeavor, which seems to be impossible in the present chaotic society and the world. Today in the periphery of educational enterprise corruptness, bribery, rivalry, political cynicism and nepotism have been omnipotent.

In any educational endeavor teacher holds a central place, he is supposed to be a role model for his students and the society but he is also an individual and human being who is greatly affected and inflicted by the vices and virtues of the human society and the world at large. Today teacher has lost his status and reverence in the society which he enjoyed in early history. Unfortunately, whole environment of the society and educational institutions is going down morally day by day. In general, man is dehumanised due to ever increasing allurements of material world and increasing desires, cut-throat competitions, declining state of social, emotional and civic security and erosion of moral and ethical values, teacher is not an exception.

Determine that things can and shall be done, and then we shall find the way.

Abraham Lincoln-

In this critical situation, can we dream of teachers who would carry Education for Peace in the realm of the classrooms? Can we dream of Teacher-Education programme that will change and educate the minds of the teachers (present and the future) who will further,

- sow the seeds of peace in the minds and souls of children;
- promote culture of peace in and out of educational institutions where our children and youth would not tend towards violence crime, depression and suicides.

Unfortunately, where most of the teachers are not serious and sincere about their professional ethics and are not aware of their role in the context of Education for Peace how can we expect that they will write the league of peace in the minds of children.

As far as Teacher-Education programmes are concerned which are planned and prepared to train teachers to deliver Education for Peace, much cannot be expected because of their theoretical and superficial nature. The Education for Peace is such enterprise which involves the desire, the spirit and the commitment of all actors pertaining to it. Today, if teacher has to be awakened to perform his role, he should be backed by appropriate training conducive environment in his institution and support of students' families and the society. All this needs a 'Will', a social will, a national will and the global will. All must join hands and hearts to realise the "will" for peace. All noble and genuine people who are willing and dreaming of better world must support education. Education is the only weapon, instead of guns, to capture the fort of peace. This is rather a last chance in human history that we cannot afford to loose. Education for

The strongest of all warriors are these two- Time and Patience.

Leo Tolstoy (War and Peace)

Peace should be taken as a joint mission of individuals, societies and nations. There are many doubts and apprehensions about education in the present chaotic and turbulent world whether it is going to change the face of world? It is a long drawn out, difficult, and at times, unrewarding combat or fight, for guns have to be silenced by ideas, but it is the last combat on which all the worlds' hopes are staked.

We must hope, out of hope that Education for Peace which seems to be a dream project of humanity today, will come out as a reality one day. Many dreams have come true in this world. All scientific inventions and discoveries are nothing but the translations of human dreams into reality. One may argue that scientists dreamt of mundane things and scientific discoveries have yielded concrete or material products which have facilitated the physical comforts of human beings. Scientific discoveries were the physical endeavors to attain the material objects but peace as an end can not be attained merely by physical endeavors. Human mind is so complex that it cannot be comforted only by food, shelter and material pleasures. If it was so why developed countries are low in Happiness Index. Thus, scientific discoveries cannot be compared with the discovery of peace in this world. The discovery of peace seems to be impossible in the present chaotic world but we should not loose hope. By educating the minds of people, we can minimise the effects and volumes of evil forces and can make the world comparatively peaceful. Today we have enough background to hope out of hope that one day our dream of peaceful world will come true, our struggle will yield the fruits of love and brotherhood one day. Today we have a great example before us how the dream of Martin Luther King, Jr which he saw forty five years ago, has come true at last in the form of Black President of United States, Barack Obama. In 1963, Martin Luther King Jr. in his speech, 'I have Dream' spoke to black Americans,

"In the process of gaining our rightful place, we must not be guilty of wrongful deeds. Let us not seek to satisfy our thirst for freedom by drinking from the cup of bitterness and hatred. ***We must forever conduct our struggle on the high plane of dignity and discipline. We must not allow our creative protest to degenerate into physical violence. Again and again, we must rise to the majestic heights of meeting physical force to soul force.***

And.. even though we face the difficulties of today and tomorrow. I still have a dream. It is a dream deeply rooted in American dream. I have a dream that one day this nation will rise up and live out the true meaning of its creed; we hold these truths to be self evident that all men are created equal. ... I have a dream that one day every valley shall be exalted and every hill and mountain shall be made low, the rough places will be made straight, and the glory of the Lord shall be revealed and all flesh shall see it together.... This is our hope and this is the faith that I go back to the South with this faith, we will be able to hew out of the mountain of despair a stone of hope, with this faith, we will be able to transform the jangling discords of our nation into a beautiful symphony of brotherhood. With this faith, we will be able to work together, to pray together, to struggle together to go to jail together, to stand up for freedom together, knowing that we will be free one day. And this will be the day when all of God's children will be able to sing with new meaning."[28]

Thus, a great faith in the dream of black people and audacity of hope have led them to freedom at last. An age old phenomenon of colour stigma has finally resolved. American people have accepted happily the leadership of black Obama and are ready to join hands and hearts to make America a better place to live. Not only Americans but the whole world is looking at Obama as if he has brought a fresh air for breath to the people of the world.

In this way, shufflings in the history of modern world show that, nothing is impossible. So we can hope again and again with this faith that Education for Peace one day will change the minds of people and the face of the world and would make the planet earth a better place to inhabit.

The struggle to build a peaceful earth should go on until such a world is achieved or until all civilisation perishes in some further war and battles of unthinkable ferocity. If there ever was a cause, if there ever can be a cause, worthy to call forth all the efforts, devotion and intelligence of men, it is the cause of peace. Organised education, a man can convince, has a significant contribution to make to that cause. The possibility of such contribution has not been clearly seen by the leaders of the nations. Now it has become imperative for them to see how this powerful force of education can be fully and wisely used in mankinds next and perhaps the last chance to build a peaceful world.

If we the people of the world, are unable to use education as the last opportunity to hold peace or we find education a failed strategy for peace, let the Education for Peace be an Utopia.

References

1. Krishnamurti, J. Living in Insane World, Seventh Talk in the Oak Grave. http//www.j.krishnamurti.org/ krishnamurti teaching/view-text.phb

2. http..devdata.worldbank. org/atlas-mdg/

3. Awake Writer (2008), Can Humans Guarantee A Happy Future? *Awake* Bangalore,The Watch Tower Bible and Tract Society of India pp. 4-5.

4. *Ibid.*

5. History's greatest monsters. http://www/ filibuster cartoons, com/monsters-htm

6. M. Bow, Amadou-Mahtar *The Will for Peace,* Address at the special (1978) session of the UN General Assembly on Disarmament, New York, UNESCO.

7. Chowdary, T.H. (1991) Gita-The Light Universal, *Bhavan's Journal,* Bombay, Bharatiya Vidya Bhavan.

8. M. Bow, Amadou. Mahtar, op. cit., p. 13.

9. Is peace really possible? The Brahma Kumaris perspective. http/ /www.the free library.com/

10. Krishnamurti, J. Self knowledge, *First and Last Freedom* http// www.j.krishnamurti.org/krishnamurti teachings/view-text.

11. Krishnamurti, J (1980), The Core of the Teachings Bibliography *About-Krishnamurti* by Mary Lutyens. http//www.j. Krishnamurti, org/about- Krishnamurti/the-core-of-the-teachings.

12. Krishnamurti. J. Self Knowledge, *First and Last Freedom* ibid.

13. Krishnamurti, ibid.

14. *UNESCO and a Culture of Peace: Promoting a Global Movement* http//www.unesco.org/general/eng/publish/ order.html

15. Stewart, R. Is Peace Achievable? What is the formula for peace? Stewart @ peace.ca.

16. *Ibid.*

17. *Ibid.*

18. *Ibid.*

19. *Ibid.*

20. *Ibid.*

21. Chopra, Deepak (2009), The soul of leadership, Education Times, *Times of India*, April 13. www.education times.com

22. M' Bow., op cit., p.15.

23. Harris, Ian M. (1988) *Peace Education.* London, Mc. Farland and company Inc. Publishers, p. 5.

24. Harris, ibid., p. 10.

25. *Ibid.*

26. *Ibid.*

27. http//www.unseco.org/general/eng/order.html.

28. Martin Luther King. Jr (1963) *I have a Dream* The coming about of the American Dream (Excerpt) Speech delivered on August 28, 1963 at the Lincoln Memorial, Washington, D.C. in The Times of India, Nov. 6, 2008. Hu.

Bibliography

BOOKS AND REPORTS

Abdul Kalam, APJ (2003), *ignited minds, unleashing the power within India,* New Delhi, Penguin Books.

Barash, P. David (2000 *Approaches to Peace*. New York, Oxford University Press.

Blavatsky, H (1981). *Practical Occcultism* Madras, The Theorophical Publishing House.

Boulding, E (1975). *The Personhood of Children* (Philadelphia PA: Religious Education Committee. Friends General Conference)

Chaudhary, S.N. (2005).(Ed) *Human Rights and Poverty in India.* Theoretical Issues and Empirical Evidences, Vol.I, New Delhi concept Publishing company.

Confederation or Confusion- Reported by Jewish War Veterans of the U.S.A. National Headquarters. Washington, D.C. 2009.

Dahl, Robert A. (1996). *Equality Verses Inequality.* Political Science and Polities.

Delors, J (1996), *Learning the Treasure within:* Report of International Commission of Education for the 21st Century, Paris, UNESCO.

Devi, R.S, *Origin, and Development of Education in India,* Vol. I, S.N. Mookerjee (ed) New Delhi, S. Chand and Company.

David, P. Barash and Charles P. Webel (2002), *Peace and Conflict Studies* Thousand Oaks, Sage Publications.

Dewey, John (1938), *Intelligence In the Modern World,* John Dewey's Philosophies Joseph Ratner (Ed.) New York, The Modern Library.

Education and the People Peace (1993), A Report of Education Policies Commission, National Education Association of United States and American Association of School Administration, Washinqton D.C.

Einstein, Albert, *On Peacre and Gandhi.* in Richard B. Gregg, Profiles in Gandhi.

Fitz. Gerald, E.*Rubaiyat of Omar Khayyam* (translation) 5th Ed.

Fountain, S (1999) *Education for Peace in UNICEF,* New York, Working Paper Education Section, Programme Divisioin, UNICEF.

Galtung, Johan (2003), *Searching for Peace-the road to TRANSCEND,* Virginia, Sterling.

Gandhi, M.K (1948) *Non violence in Pece and War.* Ahemdabad, Navajvan Publishing House.

Gangal, Anurag (1985) *New International Economic Order: Gandhian Perspective,* New Delhi.

Gangal, S.C. (1988) Gandhian Thought and Technique in the Modern World, New York, Criterion Books.

Government of India (1949). *Report of the University Education Commission (1948-49),* New Delhi; Ministry of Education, Government of India.

Government of India (1953). *Report of the secondary Education Commission* (1952-53) New Delhi, Ministry of Education, Govt. of India.

Government of India (1966) *Report of the Education Commission (1964-66) on "Education and National Development"* New Delhi, Ministry of Education, Govt. of India.

Government of India (1986), *Report of the National Policy on Education (1986)* , New Delhi, Ministry of Human Resources Development, Govt. of India.

Government of India (1993), *Learning with Burden* New Delhi, Ministry of Human Resources Development, Govt of India.

Harris, I.M. (1988) *Peace Education,* London. McFarland and Company.

Harris, I and C, McCauley (2000), *Report on the International Workshop on Education for Peace,* Israel, University of Haifa.

James and Mc Ginnis, K. (1983) *Parenting for Peace and Justice.* Maryknull, New York, Orbis Books.

Krishnamurti, J. *Total Freedom,* Chennai, Krishnamurti Foundation.

Malhotra, S., Upadhyay. P., Gupta, M., Srivastava, R., and Pandey, S. (2005) (Eds) es, *Human Rights. Emerging Issues,* New Delhi, Kilaso Books.

Mc. Bride, W.L. (1975). The Concept of Justice in Marx, Engels and others, *Ethics*, Chicago, The University of Chicago Press.

Merton, T. (1964). *Gandhi on Non-Violence,* New York New Direction.

Mitra, Veda, (1964) *Education in Ancient India* Delhi, Arya Book Depo.

Mohanty, J. (2003). *"Development of Teacher Education in India before Independence;* Teacher Education, New Delhi, Deep and Deep Publication.

Mookerjee, R.K., *Ancient Indian Education: Brahminical and Buddhist,* New Delhi Motilal Banarasi Das.

M Bow, Amadou- Mahtar (1978), *The Will For Peace* Address at the special session of the UN General Assembly on Disarmament New York, UNESCO

NCERT (2006), *National Curriculum Framework, 2005 Position Paper, National Focus Group on Education for Peace.* New Delhi. NCERT.

NCTE (1998). *Curriculum Framework for Quality Teacher Education.* New Delhi, NCTE.

Pandey, R.S. (2002), Vishwa ke Sreshtha Sisksha Shastri (GREAT EDUCATORS OF WORLD) Agra, Vinod Pustak Mandir.

Pandey S. (2004), *Education for peace, Self Instructional Package for Teacher Educators,* New Delhi, NCERT.

Ranganathananda (1986). *Eternal values for a changing society,* Bombay, Bhartiya Vidya Bhavan.

Rawls, John (1971) *A Theory of Justice,* Cambrideg: Mass.

Rearden, Betty (Ed) (1988), Education for Global Responsibility, New York, Columbia University.

Reardon, Betty & Nord land, Eva (Eds) (1994), Learning Peace, Albany, SUNY.

Rearden, Betty (1982). *Militarization, Security and Peace Education: A Guide for Concerned Citizens* (Valley forge PA: United Ministries in Education)

Richard, B, Gregg (1938) *The Power of Non Violence,* Ahemdabad, Navajeevan Publishing House.

Tagore, Ravindranath, *Gitanjali (35).*

Trever, *History of Ancient Civilisation.*

UNECO (1994) First International Forum on the Culture of Peace, San Salvador, Final Report, Paris UNESCO.

UNESCO (1977), *Thinking ahead, Unesco and the challenges of today and tomorrow,* Paris, UNESCO.

INTERNET SOURCES

About Krishnamurti at
http:.//www.j. Krishnamurti org/about-Krishanmurti/the-core-of-the-teachings-php.

A Charmed Life by Ayandrali Dutta,
Times of India, Nov. 23, 2008

Bertrand Russel
at http://www.org/wiki Bertrand Russel.

Canadian Centres for Teaching Peace
at http://www.peace.ca.

Convention of the Rights of the Child at http//en.wikipedia.org/ wik/convention on the rights of child. Newpapers (Source)

Dr. David Silvera – Mediator and trainer of mediatioj at Silvera @ sulcha.co.il

Estimalid World Wide Nuclear Stockpile at Htt//en. Wikipedia.org

Freedom From Violence Is True Liberation by J. Krishnamurti. The times of India, Allahabad, Monday, Jan 26, 2009.

Gandhi's Concept of Human Security at
http://www/scribe. com/doc/Gandhi-concept-Human-Security
http:// www/the free library.com/Mahatma Gandh+ concepts of+Global+Security+And+Peace.

Happy Planet Indes & Human Development Index. at http:// en. wikipedia. org/wiki/Happy Planet Index.

Higher Education For Peace. (2000). at
http//www.peace 2. Uit.no/hefp/contribution/papers/Ole-Mjos
http//www/times higher education. co.Uk/

History Place at
http:.//www.history place.com.
http://en. wikipedia. org/wiki

History's greatest monsters. at http:www.filibuster cartoons. com/monsters. htm.

Is Peace really possible? at
http://www. the free library, com/Is+peace+really+possible% 3f+The+BrahmaKumaris +pers.

J. Krishnamurti – You are World. at
http:// books. google.co.in/books ? id=fZu 2 AJi XY8c C&dg = j + Krishnamurti % 2B You + are + World.

J. Krishnamurit's teachings at
http://www.j.krishnamurti.org/krishnamurti-teachins/view text

Jiddu Krishnamurti at
http://en. wikipedia. org/ wiki/Jiddu-Krishnamurti

Leading by Example. by. Neerja Birla. The times of India, Monday Feb. 2, 2009.

List of Terrorist groups, at
http / / en. wiki.pedia.org / wiki
http://www.unesco,org/general/eng./publish/order.html.
http://www.unesco.org/cpp/uk/leaflet/leaf let.html.

List of staties with nucleah weapons at
http//en. wikipedia.org/wiki

Mahatma Gandhi Community Forum at
http//wwwgandhiserve.org/message.board/phpBB?view point

Military power no way to uphold human dignity
at http//www. Eurekastreet. com.au/article.appx?

New Terror Strategy by M.Bhupta and A.Pai
India Today, Dec. 8, 2008

Peace Research at
http// Jpr. Sage pub. com/egi/content/abstract

Peace at
http://www/ un.org/cyber school bus/peace/content, htm.
http:// 216.109.117.135/Search/Cache? p=peace + education

Pilgrimage to Peace by. N. Ganesh
Times of India, Nov. 4, 2008

Preampli of the Constitution of the UNESCO at www/unesco.org/education/information

Public Action. To Remedy Hunger, by Amarty Sen
at http://www/thp.org/reports/sen/sen 890, htm.

Shashi On Sunday
at http://times of india. indiatimes.com/

Striking At Will. by B. Raman
Times of India. March 15, 2008.

The Peace Formula at
http://www.peace.ca/formula.htm.

Times Foundation Sahabhagi at
http://www.times foundation. org.

The Threat Is Common. America's counter-terror strategy is flawed. by Brahma Chellaney Times of India, Feb. 6, 2009

The Coming About of The American Dream
by Martin Luther King. Jr.
Times of India, Nov. 6, 2008

The Soul of Leadership by Deepak Chopra.
Times Foundation Sahabhagi
Times of India, Education Times, April 13, 2009.

UNESCO Culture of Peace Programme
http://www/Unesco.org/cpp.
http:/www.un.org.

"UNESCO and a Culture of Peace: Promoting a Global Movement",

UNESCO Publishing. at http://www.unesco.org/general/eng/ publish/ order/html.

Universal Declaration of Human Responsibility
at http://www. asiawide.or.jp/iac/Declaration/EngDecl. htm// RESPONSIBILITIES-CITIZEN'S

Warning to All Humanity
at http://www/pgs.ca/pages/men/warning, htm.
Public trust treaty, a treaty of ethics, equity and ecology.
at http//www.gn.apc. org/negreens/cptt.htm.

Journals

Theosophical Digest, Vol. 20, No. 3 Chennai, Theosophical Publishing House. (2008).

Awake! Banglore, The Watch Tower Bible and Tract Society of India, 2008.

Journal of Peace Research, Vol. 18, No. 2
SAGE Journal on line.
http//jpr.sage, pubcom/egd/content/abstract

News Letter Vol. XXII, Jan-March Paris, IIEP, UNESCO (2004)

IIEP News Letter, Vol. XXVII, Jan-April (2009) Paris, UNESCO
Journal of Indian Education, Vol. XXXII, No.1, Feb-2007, New Delhi, NCERT.

Bhavan Journal, Vol 37, No. 31, June (1991)
Bombay, Bharatiya Vidya Bhavan

International Political Science Review, Vol 17 (1996), No.2
Gandhi Marg, Vol.25 No-4 (2004)

Journal of Peace Research, Vol. 29, Nov.3
SAGE PUBLICATION

Index

O

T

U

V